BASEBALL

...A Laughing Matter!

BASEBALL

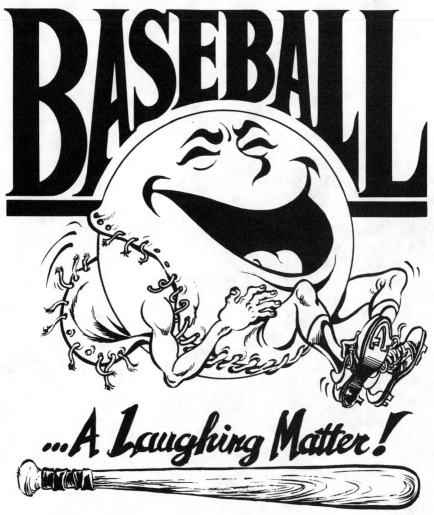

...A Laughing Matter!

by
Warner Fusselle
with
Rick Wolff and Brian Zevnik

Designed and illustrated
by

Bill Wilson

of
The Sporting News

Published in the United States by THE SPORTING NEWS Publishing Co., 1212 North Lindbergh Boulevard, St. Louis, Missouri 63132.

Library of Congress Catalog Card Number: 87-42529

ISBN: 0-89204-232-X
10 9 8 7 6 5 4 3 2 1

First Edition

CONTENTS

THE AUTHOR

Warner Fusselle, a graduate of Wake Forest University, is a Georgian who's been a baseball announcer and writer in New York City since 1977. Fusselle's announcing credits include major league baseball play-by-play, "This Week In Baseball" and national voiceovers on all major networks. Fusselle has also written a nationally syndicated newspaper column and hundreds of television programs and films on the subject of baseball.

Before moving to New York, Warner Fusselle was the play-by-play voice of the Virginia Squires in the American Basketball Association, the Richmond Braves in the Class-AAA International League and the Spartanburg Phillies in the Class-A South Atlantic League.

Rick Wolff, a former minor leaguer, and **Brian Zevnik,** a former Little Leaguer, collaborated with Warner Fusselle and lent their editorial expertise.

FOREWORD

On Sunday, June 1, 1980, I typed two pages of notes to give to a couple of my co-workers and producers of the television show "This Week in Baseball." The notes contained a Volkswagen Quiz, a Gillette Special and some of the highlights and oddities of the previous week.

A fun piece was suggested on the Los Angeles Dodgers-Cincinnati Reds game of May 27. In one inning, Dodgers pitcher Don Sutton struck out the first two batters, walked the next two, surrendered three consecutive home runs and then fanned the next batter—to strike out the side.

There also was a note on a May 28 Texas Rangers-California Angels game in which Rangers shortstop Pepe Frias tagged out the Angels' Dickie Thon and then, thinking the side was retired, rolled the ball toward the mound. But Thon represented only the second out of the inning, and Jason Thompson scored California's seventh run in a 7-6 victory.

Two weeks later these weekly notes became an official memo, and the reader list doubled to four. Each succeeding week, more and more office workers wanted a copy of what had become a very strange "This Week in Baseball" newsletter. By the end of the season, the newsletter had expanded to 11 pages and was referred to as the Fuse-Letter.

In 1981, the Fuse-Letter got its own logo and was spun off into a newspaper column available to more than 700 daily newspapers. The in-house edition continued and became zanier than ever. Then in 1982, the Fuse-Letter was transformed into one big year-end publication, and the carefully screened mailing list soon exceeded 100.

Rick Wolff, a friend of mine since our days together in the minor leagues, and his partner Brian Zevnik approached me in 1985 about turning the Fuse-Letter into the Fuse-Book. In preparation for such a book, the Fuse-Letter also became a radio spin-off in 1986 and was translated into the weekly "Fusselle File" on Mel Allen's "This Week in Baseball" national radio show. A publishing contract also was signed with The Sporting News.

In six years, two informal pages of notes have grown into thousands of pages and hours of research. The research and all-nighters were, by no means, a laughing matter. But if the final product is, then it was well worth the effort.

Warner Fusselle

Baseball players, managers, coaches and executives change teams from time to time, making it tricky to identify them when looking back through the years. Persons quoted or mentioned in this book generally are identified by the team they were with when the quote was made or the incident took place. In a few cases, other labels ("former major league pitcher," "Hall of Fame outfielder" and so on) are used when appropriate.

Managers Say the Darnedest Things

(And So Do Coaches)

Only 26 men in the entire United States can brag that they currently manage a major league baseball team. (No, Billy, it doesn't matter if you're being paid by two or three at a time!) These gentlemen are often asked for opinions on everything from religion ("I believe if God had ever managed, he would have been very aggressive, the way I manage."—Billy Martin) to history ("The Pilgrims didn't have any experience when they first arrived here. Hell, if experience was that important, we'd never have had anyone walking on the moon."—Texas Rangers rookie Manager Doug Rader) to philosophy ("Don't worry, it's gonna get worse."—Dodgers Manager Walt Alston).

Then, of course, there's baseball.

On the Managerial Roller Coaster

Rene Lachemann, Milwaukee Brewers:
"I knew there were a lot of peaks and valleys in life, but I didn't know there were so many valleys."

Billy Gardner, Minnesota Twins:
"The way things are going for me, if I'd buy a pumpkin farm, they'd cancel Halloween."

Tom Lasorda, Los Angeles Dodgers:
"I called that new president of El Salvador the other day because I wanted to talk to the only person in the world having more problems than me."

"Listen, if you start worrying about the people in the stands, before too long you're up in the stands with them."

Maury Wills, Seattle Mariners:
"People may think it's easy, but it isn't. Managing is a lonely, difficult job. It's not fun. It's a nightmare. But I enjoy it."

Pete Rose, Cincinnati Reds:
"Managing is easy. If Sparky (Anderson) can win so many games, it's got to be easy."

Paul Owens, Philadelphia Phillies:
> "The toughest part of managing is standing up for nine innings.
> It's tougher than going shopping with my wife."

Harvey Kuenn, Brewers:
> "All I do is write their names on the lineup card and let them
> play. It's not a tough job. I haven't misspelled one name yet."

Tony LaRussa (lifetime .199 batter), Chicago White Sox:
> "The toughest thing for me as a young manager is the fact that a
> lot of these guys saw me play, so it's hard for me to instruct them
> in anything because they know how bad I was."

But There's a Silver Lining

Chuck Tanner, Pittsburgh Pirates:
> "Today I have the chance to do the greatest thing anybody can
> do. I can go out and manage a winning team in the major leagues.
> Or, I can do the second-best thing anybody can do—manage a
> losing team in the major leagues."

> "People make light of my optimistic outlook, such as, if I were
> captain of the Titanic, I would tell my passengers we were stop-
> ping for ice."

> "Bill Madlock, my captain, said that he was home for a week
> following the season (in which the Pirates finished in last place)
> before he realized we weren't in the World Series."

Tom Lasorda, Dodgers:
> "I hate negativism. Every day is beautiful. When I was a kid and
> my father took his strap and was whipping my butt, I used to
> think how good it was going to feel when he stopped."

Or Maybe It's Gold

Whitey Herzog, St. Louis Cardinals:
> "The only way to make money as a manager is to win one place,
> get fired and hired somewhere else."

> "If they fire me, I'll be the highest-paid fisherman in the coun-
> try."

It Can Be Physically Trying

John Felske, Phillies:
> "I'm rapidly approaching the mentality of an ax murderer."

Jeff Newman, Oakland A's (after five games as interim manager):
> "The shock has worn off. The ulcers are setting in."

Russ Nixon, Reds:
> "This team is going to be unified—even if I have to break necks."

Casey Stengel, New York Mets:
> "Whenever I decided to release a guy, I always had his room searched first for a gun. You couldn't take chances with some of those birds."

But Honesty Is Always the Best Policy

Tom Lasorda, Dodgers:
> "I've got one fault. I lie."

Earl Weaver, Baltimore Orioles:
> "Lying always beats out the truth in this game. There's no such thing as integrity. Dishonesty is always rewarded."

Doug Rader, Rangers:
> "I usually don't give a good first impression—or a good second impression. For that matter, I usually come across like a sack of manure."

Sparky Anderson, Detroit Tigers:
> "To be honest with you, I'll be truthful."

> "You know, in this business I have to lie an awful lot. I'm not very honest with the press with all their questions because it's part of the way things are with this game."

Even If Some Feelings Get Hurt

Lee Elia, Chicago Cubs:
> "There are a lot of guys here I hope aren't here next year. You get tired of looking at garbage in your backyard."

Pat Corrales, Cleveland Indians:
> "We don't have any corked bats; we only have corked heads."

Chuck Cottier, Mariners (after cutting 12 players in spring training by erasing their names off his blackboard):
> "Ain't this some game sometimes. You work your butt off all winter, you come to camp with your hopes high and your dreams, and you get wiped out with a rolled-up sanitary sock."

Del Crandall, Mariners:
> "The one thing that has kept (second baseman Jack) Perconte from being a good major league player is performance."

Frank Robinson, Indians:
> "I had no trouble communicating. The players just didn't like what I had to say."

Billy Gardner, Twins (commenting on the 100 letters he received each day):
> "It's right down the middle. Half of them want my autograph, and the other half do not want me to pitch Ron Davis."

Joe Altobelli, Orioles:
> "There was a lot of everything in this game, including a lot of nothing."

Jerry Coleman, San Diego Padres:
"You never ask why you've been fired because if you do, they're liable to tell you."

Preston Gomez (after being fired by the Cubs in 1980):
"If everything goes right, they can win a pennant here in eight or nine years."

"Managerspeak" Can Be Tricky

Whitey Herzog, Cardinals:
"They've got to win, and we've got to win. And it's not going to rain."

Casey Stengel, Mets (at spring-training complex):
"Take those fellows over to the other diamond. I want to see if they can play on the road."

Leo Durocher, New York Giants (when asked about Bobby Thomson's famous pennant-winning home run for the Giants in the third game of the 1951 playoffs against the Brooklyn Dodgers):
"Oh, Bobby Thomson's home run? Well, that was, ah, you know, that wasn't, ah, to me, ah, eh, if you'd asked that question, I would have answered in a different way. But I'll answer it in the same way I would've answered it if you asked the question."

Harvey Kuenn, Brewers (after World Series loss):
"We're going to hang our heads high."

Billy Martin, A's (before exhibition game with the Taiyo Whales, a Japanese team):
"I don't want to make a fool of myself, but when you're out there, remember Pearl Harbor."

Tom Lasorda, Dodgers:
"A second-guesser is one who don't know anything about the first guess, and he's one who needs two guesses to get one right."

Especially When Spoken By a Manager

Tom Lasorda, Dodgers (translating a few brief comments made by pitcher Fernando Valenzuela):
"He said he likes the Dodgers, he likes Los Angeles, and he loves the managing of Tom Lasorda. He's very impressed with Lasor-

da's grasp of the game, his strategy and the way he handles pitchers."

Some Pearls From Earl

Earl Weaver will go down in history as one of the greatest and most quotable of managers. Weaver's success, however, was not foreseen by everyone. In 1968, American League umpire Bill Valentine ejected the Orioles' rookie skipper for the first time. Napp didn't think Earl would be around for too many more ejections. "You're going to be here no more than two years," he said. "Guys like you never last." (Through the 1986 season, Earl Weaver had stuck around long enough to win 1,480 games and be ejected a total of 97 times.)

Despite Weaver's success, he never really felt close to the men in blue. The men in blue felt the same way about Earl. Umpire Ron Luciano summed up the mutual feelings: "Earl and I had dinner last Sunday. He was in Florida; I was in New York. We both ate at 6:30. That's the closest we'll ever get."

Here are some bon mots from the Earl of Chesapeake:

"A manager's job is simple. For 162 games you try not to screw up all that smart stuff your organization did last December."

"The key to winning baseball games is pitching, fundamentals and three-run homers."

"I've got nothing against the bunt—in its place. But most of the time, that place is at the bottom of a long-forgotten closet."

"I never got many questions about my managing. I tried to get 25 guys who didn't ask questions."

"He (infielder Rich Dauer) has been here long enough to know he doesn't know all there is to know about what he should know."

"I'll say this: I'm getting enough money from Mr. Williams (Owner Edward Bennett Williams) that now I can pay to get my hair done if I want."

"When I left (as Orioles manager), a carton of Raleigh cigarettes was $6.50. Today it's $9.75. Who knows what it will be four years from now?"

"I don't think, in all the years I managed them, I ever spoke more than 30 words to Frank and Brooks Robinson."

Those who played for Weaver know only too well their manager's impersonal nature.

"The first time Joe (Altobelli) said hello to some guys, he broke Earl's career record."—Jim Palmer, pitcher.

"Earl is right; you can't be friends with players. And Earl manages to be unfriendly with players."—Rick Dempsey, catcher.

Dempsey had another comment about his longtime manager: "He wants the pitchers to call their own games. But if the pitcher gets hit, I get blamed."

Said Weaver: "Dempsey's ability will never continue to amaze me."

Some Gems From the Coaches

Jose Martinez, Kansas City Royals:
"Hotels have maids. Baseball teams have coaches."

Gates Brown, Tigers (on the training required to be a coach):

"In high school I took a little English, some science, some hubcaps and some wheel covers."

Richie Allen, Rangers:

"First thing I got to do is learn how to chew tobacco and get the belly out. Got to have a big belly."

Mickey Mantle, Yankees:

"I was strictly a spring-training instructor, and even then the Yankees only consulted me when they wanted to teach a kid how to strike out."

(Mantle later decided to call it quits. "I won't be back as a hitting instructor," he said, "unless I can watch Yogi give Winfield a high-five.")

Deron Johnson, Mariners:

"We're trying to get him to pull the ball once in awhile. We're not talking about 35 or 40 home runs; we're talking about him hitting more than none."

(Johnson's hitting instructions certainly worked with the above pupil, Phil Bradley. In 1984, Bradley batted .301 but did not hit even one home run. In 1985, Bradley hit .300 but also belted 26 homers.)

Art Fowler, Yankees:

"How can I make Doyle Alexander a winner? He's a great person; he makes $1.8 million. I love him. But he can't pitch."

(The Yankees agreed with pitching coach Art Fowler in 1983 and released Alexander. The Toronto Blue Jays then signed Doyle and turned him into "Alexander the Great." In 1984, Alexander went 17-6, and a year later he again won 17 games for the American League East champs.)

Joe Altobelli, Orioles:
"There was more pressure coaching third base for the Yankees than there is managing the Orioles."

Former relief pitcher Jim Brosnan once explained his impression of the coaching profession: "All coaches religiously carry fungo bats in the spring to ward off suggestions that they are not working."

The Yankees had some baserunning problems in 1982. In a game against the Twins, New York hit into a triple play. The Yankees' Graig Nettles had the perfect solution: "What we need now is a second-base coach."

Although coaches work hard and earn little pay, at least they get the respect of the players they mold into major league stars and national heroes. Nothing illustrates this better then Gary Carter's response, while still with the Expos, to coach Vern Rapp, who had offered the Montreal catcher a suggestion: "You're only a coach. I do what I want."

When the Royals signed Heisman Trophy winner Bo Jackson, they sent him to their Double-A team in Memphis to start his professional career. Minor league hitting coach Ken Berry announced his plans for helping the Royals' top prospect: "I've been told my body will be in the river if I mess with him."

After 10 years of service, John Wathan was released by the world champion Royals in 1986. Wathan was disappointed, of course, but only moments later the Royals named Wathan as their newest coach. Wathan then rendered his first comments in his new position: "The game has changed a lot since I played."

If you don't know why a coach would want to give up all of his "pressure-free" duties to occupy the hot seat of a big-league manager, A's Manager Jackie Moore set the record straight: "A coach sells cars; a manager buys them."

Giants outfielder Chili Davis in one of his hungry moments.

Baseball, Hot Dogs, Apple Pie And Stuff Away

"Some people dream of movie stars and bathing beauties. I dream of a plate of spaghetti with meatballs and sausage, and I'm eating it in my Dodger uniform."—Tom Lasorda, Los Angeles Dodgers.

The above may be Lasorda's favorite, but it's by no means the only food he will eat. Joe Torre knows the eating habits of the Dodger skipper all too well. "Tommy will eat anything as long as you pay for it," Torre said.

One thing ball players don't have to worry about is the cost of their favorite delicacy—at least for the most part. In 1983, St. Louis Cardinals rookie Andy Van Slyke had to make major adjustments in his diet when he was called up from the minor leagues. Van Slyke explained: "My biggest problem in the big leagues is that I can't figure out how to spend $43 a day in meal money."

Sometimes even the veterans forget how to budget their meal money. A good example is relief ace Goose Gossage. "I was eating out of my range," he said. "I was going to order a cheeseburger, but my wife talked me into ordering a lobster."

Pitcher Tommy John denied that he's a heavy eater. "I'm a light eater," John said. "When it gets light, I start eating."

Relief pitcher Bill Caudill started his career in the National League but then made the switch to the American League. He digested his new league this way: "The American League is like a sandwich I had for lunch—a sloppy Joe. It wasn't all that bad; there just wasn't much substance."

Although Caudill saved 36 games for the Oakland A's in 1984, that doesn't mean he was always perfect in the "Sloppy Joe League." But Bill had an explanation: "Even Betty Crocker burns a cake now and then."

Putting On the Dog

The No. 1 food at the ball park has to be the hot dog. And the hot dog is not just for the fan. Said pitcher Tug McGraw: "My favorite bull-pen was in Wrigley Field. It was right there by the same group of fans every game. You could trade baseballs for hot dogs and peanuts."

In Boston, radio announcer Andy Moss likes hot dogs but notes that they are increasingly difficult to purchase. "It now takes a 36-month payment booklet to get a hot dog and beer at Fenway Park," he said.

Pitcher Ken Brett once said that things were so bad on one of the 10 major league teams for which he pitched that the concession stands sold hot dogs *to go.*

Ball players who show off are often called hotdogs. When Dick Williams managed the San Diego Padres, his team got into a major brawl with the Atlanta Braves. Afterward, Williams didn't exactly call Braves pitcher Pascual Perez a hotdog, but he did say: "There isn't enough mustard in the state of Georgia for Mr. Perez."

New York Post columnist and radio/TV critic Phil Mushnick made this assessment of the New York Yankees' broadcast crew: "Frank conversation on Yankee broadcasts is usually limited to hot dog commercials."

Food for Thought

Major league ball players have access to quite a spread of food in the clubhouse for after-game munching. The menu is usually just what the players order, so you can imagine the reaction of the Texas Rangers when they found the following bulletin on the clubhouse wall: "In an attempt to eliminate nutritional habits that are counterproductive to achieving the maximum level of physical conditioning, we would like you to consider after-game food such as fruit juice, fruit nectar, fresh fruit, iced tea, soup, green salad, cottage chesse, yogurt, tuna salad, precooked ham and wheat bread."

Don't dismiss the above menu until you've had a chance to sample the delights of press box chow. Cardinals announcer Jack Buck had this warning regarding the cuisine in the press box in Atlanta: "You have to have a sense of humor to eat here. The food tastes funny."

Most baseball fans like, on occasion, beans and franks. But history

also notes a "beaned Frank." It seems that on May 30, 1904, the Chicago Cubs' Frank Chance was hit by a pitch five times in a double-header.

Wade Boggs of the Boston Red Sox is known as "The Chicken Man" because he eats chicken every day. The third baseman even put out a book of his favorite recipes called "Fowl Tips."

Speaking of recipes, Cardinals pitcher Danny Cox has a favorite of his own—"Danny Cox's Fettucini Almost-Alfredo."

Eating Out of Their League

Pitcher Pedro Borbon had some peculiar eating habits during his days with the Cincinnati Reds. During a brawl, Pedro once tried to eat an opponent's cap. In the Dominican Republic during winter ball one year, Borbon picked up a black cat and threw it to the catcher. "I should have eat it," he later commented. Borbon also was accused of biting a bouncer at a nightclub.

In more recent times, Atlanta Braves second baseman Glenn Hubbard once grabbed a moth out of the air and then proceeded to eat it. (This

is the same Glenn Hubbard who once modeled a snake around his neck while posing for his official baseball-card photograph.)

Relief pitcher Jim Kern once ate the notes taken by a sportswriter. This incident occurred right after it was mentioned to Kern that he might have to eat his words. On another occasion, Kern ate the last 10 pages of a book that was being read by a sportswriter on an airplane. Kern had a logical explanation: "Why not? I once ate part of The Sporting News."

Brad (the Animal) Lesley of the Reds was another pitcher who enjoyed newspaper columns—eating them, that is. On one occasion, the Animal threatened to go straight for the source: "You tell that writer that if he comes around here, I'm going to chew his arm off."

Manager Gene Mauch of the California Angels wanted outfielder Brian Downing to lead off in the batting order. Downing let it be known that he preferred to bat elsewhere. Mauch got the message. "Brian would rather eat a green fly than lead off," he said.

A's slugger Dave Kingman had some advice for umpire Steve Palermo and his eating habits. Kong's tactful suggestion: "He has the worst breath I've ever heard, er, the worst breath I've ever seen. Hell, he shouldn't eat so much garlic."

Diet Delights

Portly pitcher Sid Fernandez of the New York Mets has to keep an eye on his waistband year-round. El Sid counts the calories by putting mustard on his baked potato instead of sour cream or butter.

Frank Robinson once lost 22 pounds on a grapefruit diet. "After four days you're hallucinating," he said, "and after a week you want to go

out and find a grapefruit farmer and blow his head off."

Reliever Terry (Goo) Forster controls his weight with this philosophy: "If it tastes good, spit it out."

Yogi Berra even diets from time to time. "I'll have some french fries," he tells the waitress, "but no potatoes because I'm on a diet."

Yogi also counts his calories when he asks the clubhouse man for something to drink: "Hey, Nick, get me a diet Tab."

Sweet PUN-ishment

Years ago, Reggie Jackson said that if he played in New York, he'd have a candy bar named after him. On November 29, 1976, Reggie signed with the Yankees as a free agent. Shortly thereafter, the Reggie! bar was unveiled.

Yankees Owner George Steinbrenner felt responsible. "With the money I'm paying him," he said, "they should have named a candy bar after me." And thus, the Payday?

Just think, if:

- ■ Mickey Mantle and Roger Maris had ever played in New York, someone probably would have introduced M&Ms.

- ■ catcher Mike Heath had stayed with the Yankees for more than 33 games, there probably would have been a Heath bar.

- ■ utilityman Bill Almon had stuck with the Mets for more than 48 games, there could have been an Almon Joy.

- ■ Mets pitcher Dwight Gooden keeps up his flamethrowing, there may be a candy bar called Gooden Plenty.

- ■ America's team, the Braves, ever develops a staff of great pitchers, there could even be a candy bar called Mounds.

Sweet Dreams

Naming a candy bar after a sports star or celebrity is not as easy as it may seem. Politics plays a major role in the decision-making process. This fact was never more evident than during the International Conference of Confection, better known as the ICC.

The United States and Japan were selected to head the conference and its naming of an international candy bar. The U.S. wanted to name the candy bar after its all-time home run king, Henry Aaron. Japan wanted to name it after the great Japanese slugger, Sadaharu Oh. Because these players were the two greatest home run hitters in baseball history, it was no easy decision. A compromise was needed to appease both of these powerful countries. The first suggestion, a Sadaharu Aaron bar, was voted down. But after much deliberation, a settlement produced the internationally acclaimed Oh Henry candy bar. (Snickers, Snickers, Snickers . . .)

Fast Food

In 1984, the Mets had a minor league prospect named Gene Autry who played at Little Falls in the New York-Penn League. Autry did commercials for Roy Rogers.

This endorsement was not unprecedented in the Mets' organization. Two years earlier, Ronald MacDonald played for the Mets' Triple-A farm team at Tidewater in the International League. MacDonald did commercials for Burger King. (Ronald had previously worked at McDonald's, where he met his wife.)

In 1985, pitcher Don Sutton finally signed with the A's after stating on numerous occasions that he would prefer to play elsewhere. Sutton's new teammate, Mike Norris, explained the surprise signing thusly: "This isn't Burger King. You can't have it your way."

Minor League Munchies

If fast food is important to major leaguers, you can imagine how terribly important it is to all the young players in the minor leagues. For a minor leaguer, a balanced meal is a hot dog in each hand.

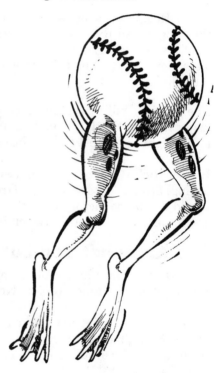

Outfielder Allan Peterson, who played in the Angels' farm system in 1984 and '85, established a reputation as a big eater long before he began his minor league career. In 1979, at the age of 17, Peterson made the Guinness Book of World Records by eating 20¾ hamburgers and buns in 30 minutes. (His record stood for seven years before being broken in 1986.)

The Baltimore Orioles signed a young pitching prospect named Rick Rice and sent him off to the minor leagues. Rick's last name fits in here nicely, but his diet did not consist of rice while playing baseball. "I always eat frog legs before I pitch," he explained. "It makes my fastball jump."

Double Snack Attack

Infielder Joe Morgan had a peculiar way of describing one of his great seasons with the Reds: " '75 was very rewarding for me because I won MVP and we won a world championship. Rose and Perez had been on the team and won MVPs, but they didn't win world championships. It's like double gravy on the cake."

Joseph Epstein, editor of American Scholar, tried to explain the relationship between baseball and business after the 1981 players strike. "Sports and business go together like oysters and chocolate sauce," he wrote. "That is to say, not very palatably."

In 1983, catcher Junior Ortiz hit .249 in 73 games with the Pittsburgh Pirates and the Mets. Late in the year with the Mets, Ortiz hit a double, although Junior wasn't satisfied. "If I'd had another glass of orange juice, that ball would have been out of here," he said.

The Orioles' Tito Landrum hit a clutch home run in the 10th inning of the fourth and final game of the 1983 A.L. Championship Series against the Chicago White Sox. Tito described his heroic homer: "The pitch was a fastball, dead in the middle of the plate—ice cream."

When Reggie Jackson was asked about batting against the hard-throwing Nolan Ryan, he cited one of his favorite desserts to explain what it was like: "Every hitter likes fastballs, just like everybody likes ice cream. But you don't like it when someone's stuffing it into you by the gallon."

The Pirates' Willie Stargell described his 21st and final season in the major leagues thusly: "I look at my career and savor it like a good meal. Right now I feel I'm on the dessert."

Pitcher Rich Bordi of the Yankees called on an edible to describe his feelings after a sensational Ken Griffey catch in the ninth inning preserved a Yankee victory over the Red Sox: "Heck, this game was so great, even the coleslaw in the clubhouse afterward looked good."

You Are What You Eat

Jeff Stone of the Philadelphia Phillies was asked if he would like a shrimp cocktail. Stone's reply: "No thanks, I don't drink."

There apparently are not too many Jeff Stones who hang out in the bleachers of Chicago's Wrigley Field. In one game, 3,200 fans were in the bleachers for a Cubs game. In nine innings they bought 5,600 beers and 17 soft drinks.

A's pitcher Mike Norris was tested for drugs in 1985, and the test showed traces of alcohol and codeine. Norris explained the test results by saying that he had eaten shrimp cooked in wine for lunch.

Relief pitcher Tom Niedenfuer assessed the ability of the Dodgers' bullpen. "I think our relievers are a lot like peanut butter and jelly," he said. "We're better as a group than we are separately."

Chicago White Sox rookie slugger Ron Kittle was asked about his

A weighty meeting at home plate.

impressions of New York after visiting the city in 1983. Kittle's re-sponse: "The only thing I found difficult about New York was enjoy-ing a $20 omelette."

Detroit Tigers Manager Sparky Anderson commented on the need for a pitcher to eat: "I don't think you should throw at anyone's head, but you ought to be able to crack some ribs. A pitcher's got to eat. Don't they have a right to move the hitter off the plate?"

When San Francisco Giants catcher Bob Brenly was asked to appraise the appearance of his new teammate, pitcher Juan Berenguer, he ap-parently had food on his mind. "If I drove up to a restaurant and he was doing the valet parking, I'd go somewhere else to eat," he joked.

Because any discussion of food on the major league level begins with Tom Lasorda—he has been seen wearing a T-shirt that says "Please Don't Feed The Manager"—perhaps it should end with the Dodger skipper, too:

> *"When we win, I'm so happy I eat a lot. When we lose, I'm so depressed I eat a lot. And when we're rained out, I'm so disappointed I eat a lot."*

The Best Pitcher on Pluto

Up Close
And Personal

ANDUJAR, JOAQUIN

Born December 21, 1952—San Pedro de Macoris, Dominican Republic. Height: 6'0". Weight: 180 lbs. Throws: Right. Bats: Both. Signed by the Cincinnati Reds on November 14, 1969. Traded to the Houston Astros on October 24, 1975. Traded to the St. Louis Cardinals on June 7, 1981. Traded to the Oakland A's on December 10, 1985.

Wacky Joaquin is one tough Dominican—at least in his opinion. And he must be or else he wouldn't have become a two-time 20-game winner in the National League, nor would he have led the Cardinals to two World Series and pitched for the National League in the 1979 All-Star Game. Becoming a well-known major league pitcher represents a great deal of success, especially for one who had to quit school in the Dominican Republic because he didn't even own a pair of shoes.

Andujar will never forget his background: "We play in the streets. We don't come from college where they have a bat, a glove and a coach. In San Pedro de Macoris, they have only me."

Joaquin loves to play, and that doesn't mean that he merely loves to pitch. Andujar loves to hit as much, if not more, than he loves to pitch. And he's a switch-hitter, although he doesn't always bat righthanded against lefties and lefthanded against righthanders. Joaquin's Cardinal teammate, pitcher Bob Forsch, explained: "If I know Joaquin, he probably doesn't know which way he's batting until he grabs his batting helmet. Depending on which side the flap is, that's how he bats."

Cardinals Manager Whitey Herzog always defended his ace pitcher, but there were times when it was not easy. "He earns a million dollars a year for pitching," he said. "I ought to get a million for managing him."

Joaquin may never be compared to Plato or Aristotle, but when Andujar philosophizes, you can't help but listen:

(About the weather):
    "You can't worry if it's cold. You can't worry if it's hot. You only worry if you get sick. Because then if you don't get well, you die."

(About fans):
"They think they pay our salaries, but what about Pittsburgh? Nobody goes to the stadium there, and the players still get paid."

(About homesickness):
"It's great to finally be home. It seems as if we've been gone for five weeks." (Counting spring training and a road trip, the Cardinals had actually been gone for seven weeks.)

(About the dangers of pitching):
"I throw the ball 92 miles an hour, but they hit it back just as hard."

(After a slump-ending victory):
"God is back in the National League. Matter of fact, he is staying at my house. I'll have to have a barbecue for him."

(About his intelligence):
"How can I play baseball if I'm stupid? If I was stupid, I wouldn't have pitched in the World Series. I'd be playing ball in Mexico or Yugoslavia or on Pluto."

(About the media):
"I will talk to you guys (sportswriters) tomorrow—after I see what you write tomorrow."

(About pitching to himself):
"I'd throw me a fastball right down the middle. What do you think, I'm gonna try and get myself out?"

(About playing at Wrigley Field):
"It's hard to see the ball in the daytime here."

(About American League stadiums and rules):
"The stadiums in the American League are softball stadiums."

"When I saw the left-field fence (at Fenway Park in Boston), I thought we were going to play softball."

"I would hit 15 to 20 home runs if they let me DH here (Minnesota's Metrodome). Even the little midget (Ozzie Smith) would hit 25 home runs here."

"The DH is a 10th player. Softball is 10 guys. Baseball is nine."

(About pitching to George Brett of the Kansas City Royals):
"I pitch him like a softball pitcher. I am just going to throw him my best pitch and let him hit it. He's going to hit it anyway. He can hit a home run anytime he wants to. I can tell when he's trying to hit a home run. This is my secret, and I cannot tell you."

(After showing disinterest in a stretching drill):
"Babe Ruth never stretched."

(About the highs and lows of his major league career):
"Baseball can be summed up by one word: 'You never know.' "

BERRA, LAWRENCE PETER

Born May 12, 1925—St. Louis. Height: 5'8". Weight: 191 lbs. Throws: Right. Bats: Left. Played with the New York Yankees from 1946-63; player/coach in 1963. Manager of the Yankees in 1964. Player/coach with the New York Mets in 1965. Mets coach from 1966-71. Manager of the Mets from 1972-75. Yankees coach from 1976-83. Manager of the Yankees from 1984-85. Coach with the Houston Astros in 1986.

At age 19, Lawrence Peter Berra was a Seaman 2nd Class in the U.S. Navy. On D-Day, June 6, 1944, Berra and company were lending anti-aircraft support to the invasion of Normandy. They were right on target in their attempt to shoot down a low-flying plane. But there was one problem: The plane they shot down turned out to be American. An angry but uninjured pilot was fished out of the water while screaming at the top of his lungs: "If you shot down as many of theirs as you shot down of ours, the war would have been over a long time ago!"

Two years later, Yogi Berra was in the major leagues as a rookie catcher for the Yankees. Berra was fortunate to have one of the game's greatest catchers of all time show him the ropes. "Bill Dickey is learning me his experience," Yogi explained.

Yogi played in 15 All-Star Games and 75 World Series games, won the American League Most Valuable Player award three times, managed pennant winners in both leagues and was inducted into the Hall of

Fame. But he is best remembered for his myriad malapropisms, which left folks scratching their heads.

To wit:

"I never blame myself when I'm not hitting. I just blame the bat, and if it keeps up I change bats. After all, if I know it isn't my fault that I'm not hitting, how can I get mad at myself?"

"How can I hit and think at the same time?"

"So I'm ugly. So what? I never saw anyone hit with his face."

"You give 100 percent in the first half of the game, and if that isn't enough, in the second half you give what's left."

"Ninety percent of this game is half mental."

"You observe a lot just by watching."

"If the people don't want to come out to the park, nobody's going to stop 'em."

"You've got to be very careful if you don't know where you are going because you might not get there."

"A nickel ain't worth a dime anymore."

"Nobody goes there anymore. It's too crowded."

"I take a two-hour nap from 1 o'clock to 4."

"What's the saying? Don't look a good thing in the eye?"

"If you ask me something I don't know, I'm not gonna answer."

"This is the earliest I've ever been late."

"We made too many wrong mistakes."

"Uniforms are all the same. Some are just hotter than others."

"I think Little League is wonderful. It keeps the kids out of the house."

Tailgunner Berra

"It's deja vu all over again."

Yogi Sets Heads of State Spinning

Yogi was invited to the White House for dinner, but he was a little confused about the menu. "I thought they said *steak* dinner," he said, "but then I found out it was a *state* dinner."

"I think I'm one of the few sports people that's going to be there," Yogi remarked. "They're honoring some oil king." (The guest to whom Yogi was referring was King Hussein of Jordan.)

"Not much," replied Yogi when asked what the President said to him. "You couldn't keep a conversation going because everybody was talking too much."

Yogi also met the Pope.

> Interviewer: "I understand you had an audience with the Pope."
> Yogi: "No, but I saw him."
> Interviewer: "Did you get to talk to him?"
> Yogi: "I sure did. We had a nice little chat."
> Interviewer: "What did he say?"
> Yogi: "You know, he must read the papers a lot, because he said, 'Hello, Yogi.'"
> Interviewer: "And what did you say?"
> Yogi: "I said, 'Hello, Pope.'"

When introduced to writer Ernest Hemingway, Yogi is reported to have gotten up to shake Hemingway's hand and said, "What paper you write for, Ernie?"

The Post-Playing Days Yogi

When Yogi's playing days ended, his quotable days were just beginning. Whether as manager or coach, Yogi Berra's words of wisdom were always welcome.

Such as:
> "All I know is that my players are frosting at the bit."

> "A home opener is always exciting, no matter whether it's at home or on the road."

"A three-game series at the beginning of the season is longer than a three-game series in July."

(After winning the first two games of a three-game series):
"I think we have a better chance of sweeping this series than they do."

(About outfielder Rickey Henderson):
"He can run anytime he wants. I'm giving him the red light."

(About pitcher Ray Fontenot):
"Every time he loses, he's got a better chance of winning his next time out."

(During a postgame interview):
"I wish I had an answer for that because I get tired of answering that question."

(About the 1954 Cleveland Indians, who won 111 games and the A.L. pennant):
"Bobby Avila had a good year for them. He got the MVP that year, I think. 1954? I'm pretty sure. Didn't he?"
(Sorry, Yogi, but the 1954 MVP award went to the Yankees' hard-hitting catcher—Yogi Berra.)

(About Yankees Owner George Steinbrenner):
"Well, we agree different."

Non-Baseball Yogiisms

(On the golf circuit):
"Ninety percent of the putts that fall short of the cup don't go in."

(About his sweater collection):
"The only color I don't have is navy brown."

(When asked about the kind of house he had just purchased):
"I don't know, but it's full of rooms."

(About getting keys out of a locked car):
"You gotta call a blacksmith."

(About Steve McQueen's role in "The Magnificent Seven"):
   "He made that movie before he died."

(Reaction to his wife, Carmen, who told him that she had just seen "Doctor Zhivago"):
   "Oh, what's the matter with you now?"

(About his reputation as a master of the malaprop):
   "I didn't say everything I said."

QUISENBERRY, DANIEL RAYMOND

Born February 7, 1953—Santa Monica, Calif. Height: 6'2". Weight: 180 lbs. Throws: Right. Bats: Never. Signed as a free agent by the Kansas City Royals on June 7, 1975.

Relief pitcher Dan Quisenberry has defied all odds in the game of baseball. First of all, no major league team wanted him when he got out of high school. And few teams were interested when he got out of college. It also should be noted that he doesn't throw very hard, nor does he throw in an orthodox fashion. Dan Quisenberry throws underhanded, just like your sister did in first grade.

Nevertheless, Quiz became the first relief pitcher in baseball history to win five Rolaids Fireman of the Year awards. From 1982-85, Quisenberry led the American League in saves each year, posting save totals of 35, 45, 44 and 37.

But enough about the pitching of Dan Quisenberry. Quiz is not just another piece of meat to throw out on the mound. He's a person, a human being. He has a family, a mind, a life away from baseball; most of all, Dan Quisenberry has something to say. So say it, Quiz.

Some Q-Tips

(Generally speaking):
   "Most pitchers fear losing their fastball, and since I don't have one, the only thing I have to fear is fear itself."

   "They ought to trade me for the seven hostages left in Lebanon. I deserve to be locked up more than they do. Whether Ronald Reagan can work that out or not, I don't know."

   "If we come back and win this thing, it'll be like finding Amelia

Wading in, Not Walking on

Earhart out on a date with Jimmy Hoffa."

"I broke my slump when I found a delivery in my flaw."

"(Yankees Owner) George Steinbrenner has one simple ambition in life. He just wants all the land next to his."

"Reggie Jackson hit one (home run) off me in Kansas City that's still burrowing its way to St. Louis."

(About his role in a brawl between the Royals and the Red Sox):
"I was looking for the calmest guy on the field. The whole thing reminded me of the junior prom—not a lot of action, just a lot of guys standing around, watching what's going on."

(About playing the division-rival California Angels in the last week of the season):
"The only electricity here tonight was in the lights."

(More about the Angels):
"They're like the American League All-Star team, and that's their problem. The American League All-Star team always loses."

(About the 1982 Milwaukee Brewers and the All-Star Game):
"We should simply have sent the Brewers out there. The National League would have taken one look at them and conceded. There's no quiche eaters among their starting lineup."

(About pitching in relief):
"We're parasites. We live off the people who spend two hours on the field."

"A manager uses a relief pitcher like a six-shooter. He fires until it's empty and then takes the gun and throws it at the villain."

"I'm not a Mercedes. I'm a Volkswagen. They get a lot of mileage out of me, but I'm not pretty."

More Quiz-Biz

(About the 1981 baseball strike):
"I think it's basically like any labor problem; nobody talks about

it until the last minute. If it's trash, you wait until the stink gets too bad. If it's coal, you wait until black lung disease sets in. If it's nuclear energy, you wait until Joan Baez shows up."

(About playing while star third baseman George Brett was injured):
"Our goal is to get as many games rained out as we can."

(About smoothing out the infield in Oakland to eliminate bad hops):
"Well, I've always been partial to getting a dead whale and rolling it over the dirt. Really works. Of course, it's smelly, and a lot of people don't like it."

(About the Metrodome in Minnesota):
"There's no lead safe in this yard. There's no fail-safe zone. It's Condition Red all the time."

"I don't think there are good uses for nuclear weapons, but this place might be one."

(About his "slump" in 1985):
"For the last few years, I could walk on water. This year I got wet."

"If I stink every year and get 37 saves, I'll be pretty happy stinking."

(About putting a lot of runners on base in early 1986):
"My job is to keep people in the park for the concessionaires. They love me. I make the game exciting."

(About finding out that he no longer would be used only in late-inning relief):
"There will be some adjustments I'll have to make. I'll have to get used to tying my shoes earlier in the game."

KEARNEY, ROBERT HENRY

Born October 3, 1956—San Antonio. Height: 6'0". Weight: 185 lbs. Throws: Right. Bats: Right. Selected by the San Francisco Giants in the 14th round of the free-agent draft on June 7, 1977. Drafted from the Giants by the Oakland A's on December 9, 1980. Traded to the Seattle Mariners on November 21, 1983.

Bob Kearney made his major league debut in 1979 with the Giants, but he played briefly in only two games. Bob did not become a legend until he joined the A's and became their regular catcher in 1983.

Catch-23: During one game in the '83 season, covering a span of only 23 pitches, Kearney showed that he was a facile learner. He called for 15 consecutive fastballs, so the A's pitching coach, Ron Schueler, went to the mound with some wise advice: "Why not mix it up a little, Bob?" Kearney heeded his mentor and promptly changed the pitching pattern. He called for eight straight curveballs.

If that doesn't seem like a particularly intelligent decision, Kearney, a good defensive catcher, has the perfect defense for such charges: "Hey, there are different kinds of intelligence. Albert Einstein was bad in English; of course, Einstein was German."

Kearney has also been known to speak in other tongues. Although he was Seattle's starting catcher in 1984, Bob had to sit when Salome Barojas was on the mound. Of course, Kearney kept cool; he understood the reasoning behind such a move, which allowed Orlando Mercado to catch Barojas. "I don't speak Spanish," he said. "C'est la vie."

Kearney is not afraid to speak out to the umpires when he believes his team has been slighted. In one game Bob let the umpire know he had blown the call on what should have been a foul ball. Kearney had proof that the ball was foul and let the umpire know: "The ball hit the foul part of the bag!"

When Special K went to Yankee Stadium in New York and saw all the monuments in the outfield, he was amazed. "There's not enough room for that many people to be buried here," he remarked.

Bob, who always tries to stay in good condition, doesn't drink tea or coffee. That's because they have "too much nicotine."

In 1985, Kearney's second season with the Mariners, he got off to a terrible start with the bat. The 28-year-old catcher got a hit in the Mariners' first game of the year but then went into a slump. By the end of April he still was looking for his second hit, and his batting average dropped to .029. Kearney was quite worried and expressed his concern: "I'm getting close to hitting my age." (Bob finally got out of his slump and hit .269 for the rest of the season to end the year at .243.)

"King Solomon" Kearney

Earning His Appellation

If you still aren't sure how Bob Kearney became Special K, here are a few more examples of catcher Kearney at his best.

Kearney explained an opponent's extra-base hit in the Kingdome in Seattle by saying: "It was a wind-blown double."

When getting ready to play the Baltimore Orioles and hearing that the great Jim Palmer would be on the mound, Kearney asked: "Is Palmer righthanded or lefthanded?"

Kearney and his teammates were getting ready to play the Boston Red Sox when someone brought up the name of the legendary Carl Yastrzemski. Bob was confused. "Yastrzemski?" he asked. "Wasn't he traded to the Orioles?"

In 1984, the Detroit Tigers won 35 of their first 40 games, achieving one of the best starts in baseball history. Many words were written about the peerless Tigers, but perhaps Kearney said it best: "This might be a game of inches, but the Tigers have all the inches right now. They own the yardstick."

RIVERS, JOHN MILTON

Born October 31, 1948—Miami. Height: 5'10". Weight: 162 lbs. Throws: Left. Bats: Left. Selected by the Atlanta Braves in the secondary phase of the free-agent draft on June 5, 1969. Traded to the California Angels on September 8, 1969. Traded to the New York Yankees on December 11, 1975. Traded to the Texas Rangers on August 1, 1979. Released April 1, 1985.

John Milton Rivers played 15 poetic seasons in the major leagues and compiled a .295 lifetime batting average. He also played in three World Series and one All-Star Game and led the American League in stolen bases one season with 70. None of this means anything, however, unless you know that John Milton Rivers is really Mickey Rivers.

Mick the Quick can no longer be found in daily box scores, but he's not easily forgotten. Although he never owned his own bat, Ole Gozzlehead certainly made his mark on the national pastime.

"Ain't no sense in worrying about things you got control

Checking the Wind-Chill Factor

over, 'cause if you got control over them, ain't no sense worrying. And there ain't no sense worrying about things you got no control over, 'cause if you got no control over them, ain't no sense worrying about them."—Mickey Rivers.

More From Mick the Quip

(Generally speaking):
"We'll do all right if we capitalize on our mistakes."

"My goals are to hit .300, score 100 runs and stay injury-prone."

"I might have to commute. You know, left field, DH, wherever."

"What was the name of that dog on 'Rin Tin Tin?' "

(About the physical looks of other players):
"The ugliest player I ever saw was Danny Napoleon. He was so ugly that when you walked by, your clothes would wrinkle."

"He (former teammate Cliff Johnson) is so ugly he should have to wear an oxygen mask."

(After playing left field for the first time):
"I felt alone out there, like I was on a desert island. I felt like Gilligan."

(About the weather):
"The first thing you do when you get out to center field is put your finger up and check the wind-chill factor."

"The wind was blowing 100 degrees."

"I didn't want the wind to hit me, so I tried to outrun the wind."

"It was so cold today that I saw a dog chasing a cat, and the dog was walking."

"I was brought up in Florida, so there isn't much difference between playing there and here. The climax are about the same."

(About a teammate who had just played his first game):
"He was lost out there. He was the Lost Mohegan."

(About teammates Bill Stein and Larry Biittner):
"These guys are so old they're eligible for Meals on Wheels."

(After hitting a double off Boston's Bob Stanley):
"That felt good. I hadn't hit off a lefty in two months." (Bob Stanley is righthanded.)

(After teammate Buddy Bell threw three helmets in a game, Mickey presided over the Rangers' kangaroo court):
"That's three helmets at two dollars a helmet. Three and two is five, so you owe five dollars, Buddy."

(After announcing that someday he plans to join Billy Martin and George Steinbrenner and manage the Yankees):
"Oh, George understands me. Me and him and Billy, we're two of a kind."

John Butcher was one of Mickey's teammates in Texas when he pitched a one-hitter for the Rangers. Butcher then made this analysis:
"I threw about 90 percent fastballs and sliders. Fifty percent fastballs and 50 percent sliders. Hey, wait, I'm starting to sound like Mickey Rivers."

Dodgers rooter Hilda Chester and cowbell.

Ladies Day

(Foul Balls and the Fair Sex)

Dear Ann Landers: I've been away playing baseball for five months. Last week I sent my wife a telegram saying I'd be home in three days. But when I walked in, I found her in the arms of my best friend. Tell me, Miss Landers, what made her do such an awful thing?
Dear Sir: Maybe she didn't get your telegram.

From Hilda To Morganna

Perhaps the best-known fan of all time was Brooklyn Dodgers booster Hilda Chester. It was Hilda who made the cowbell famous at the ball park. It just wasn't baseball in Brooklyn without Hilda Chester and her cowbell in the center-field bleachers at Ebbets Field. Those bleachers may not have offered the best vantage point in the house, but they were close enough to get Hilda involved in just about everything. And that included managing.

It was the early 1940s and Pistol Pete Reiser was in center field. Legend has it that Hilda wrote a note and threw it into the outfield near Reiser. She instructed Pete to give it to Manager Leo Durocher the next inning. Reiser put the note into his pocket without reading it, and then after the third out he headed for the Dodger dugout. On the way in, Pete greeted Brooklyn General Manager Lee MacPhail, who had waved from his box seat next to the dugout. Reiser then proceeded to the dugout and gave Hilda's note to the Dodger manager.

In the next inning, Durocher promptly yanked the Dodger pitcher, who had been pitching well, and brought in a reliever who almost blew the game. Afterward, the volatile Durocher was ready to explode. He went over to Reiser and instructed him never to bring him another note from MacPhail during a game. Reiser informed a stupefied Leo that the note containing pitching instructions came not from MacPhail, but from the center-field bleachers and a most concerned fan: Hilda Chester.

"I kiss them on the cheek because I hate chewing tobacco. And when the cops are chasing you, you don't have time to find out if a guy is chewing bubble gum or tobacco."—Morganna Roberts, the Kissing Bandit (60-24-39).

On opening day at the Kingdome in Seattle in 1986, the Mariners'

Morganna Roberts, alias the Kissing Bandit.

newly acquired catcher, Steve Yeager, became yet another victim of the Kissing Bandit, Morganna Roberts. Seattle was the 19th team that the generously endowed stripper had conquered since 1970, when her first victim was Cincinnati's Pete Rose. Morganna vows that she won't strike any team a second time until she's done all 26 teams once, although she made one player—George Brett of the Kansas City Royals—a two-time buss recipient.

Another one of Morganna's indoor victims was Houston Astros pitcher Nolan Ryan. Local authorities at the Astrodome were not very understanding, however, and wanted to press charges. Morganna's attorney explained that she had hurtled over the railing and onto the field because of "an imbalance created by the force of gravity."

Morganna's lawyer is very important to her because she insists she wouldn't look good in prison stripes. "They make me look top-heavy," she said.

Since Morganna is so sensitive about her figure, she was not too fond of her latest measurements: "I've gained an inch around the waist."

One of Morganna's successful conquests was the California Angels. But for the Angels' Bobby Grich, it was more an embarrassment. "I was on deck one day, and Morganna came out of the stands. I started to reach for her, and she ran right by me and kissed Fred Lynn."

Lynn was even more embarrassed. After being embraced and graced by a kiss, Fred struck out with the bases loaded. Lynn rationalized afterward: "She had me surrounded. After looking at her chest, it made the ball look like a pencil dot."

Of Wives and Lovers

After more than three decades of marriage, Los Angeles Dodgers Manager Tom Lasorda was not ashamed to express his love for his wife, Joan.

> Joan: "I think you love baseball more than you love me."
> Tom: "Yeah, but I love you more than I love football and basketball."

New York Mets announcer Ralph Kiner showed his sentiments for baseball wives during a broadcast while talking about pitcher Jerry

Koosman. "This is one of the class guys in the game," Kiner said. "And he has a great wife—if there is such a thing as a great wife."

New York Yankees fan Cliff Donadio will not take his wife to a baseball game because of something she did, or actually didn't do, in 1969. On Mickey Mantle Day, she *didn't cry.*

Baltimore Orioles Manager Earl Weaver did his best to be a good husband, but his devotion to baseball was evident. "I gave Mike Cuellar more chances than my first wife," he said, "and I've given Alan Wiggins more chances than Cuellar."

Outfielder Paul Householder got engaged on New Year's Eve in 1982 after a season in which he batted only .211 with the Cincinnati Reds. Paul explained his engagement: "With the kind of year I had, I'm ready to try anything."

Although it was not a shotgun wedding, Pete Rose was "forced" to get married in 1984. "I had to get married," he said, "because that was the only way I could get her on the team plane back to Montreal. Only wives are allowed."

Art Rust Jr. is a noted New York City sports talk-show host and author. Art and Edna Rust were married in 1952 and had 34 years together before Mrs. Rust died in 1986. Art once took Edna to a baseball game at the Polo Grounds when they were dating. Edna looked out onto the infield dirt and asked: "What's that white rag on the field?" An amused Art responded: "Baby, that white rag is second base."

For some reason, baseball wives don't always believe their husbands. After working overtime in a minor league game that was suspended after 32 innings, pitcher Luis Aponte rushed straight home to see his wife, where she greeted him with a strange look. "My wife said, 'Where have you been?'" Aponte recalled, "and I said, 'At the ball park.' She said, 'You're lying.'"

Baseball Commissioner Happy Chandler made a pledge to his wife when he got married: "I promised that if we ever fussed, I would go outside. Fifty-seven years in the open air does wonders for a man's health."

Behind Every Great Man Is. . .

Relief pitcher Tug McGraw's wife was responsible for one of baseball's most recognized mannerisms—Tug's slapping his glove on his leg after getting the final out of the inning. "Funny how that started," McGraw said. "After a game once, my wife, Phyllis, mentioned she always was concerned how I was feeling. I told her when everything was OK, I'd slap my glove and she'd know. I've never stopped doing that."

Ray Knight of the Mets is not the only celebrity in his household. Ray is married to star golfer Nancy Lopez. It seems that Knight's thoughts are not always on baseball. "If it weren't for the money," he said, "I'd retire and go caddie for my wife."

Tim Flannery of the San Diego Padres also thinks of other sports from time to time. "If I had to leave the game," he said, "I'd surf all day and become a professional go-getter. My wife would go to work, and I'd go get 'er."

The Chicago Cubs' Bob Dernier expressed the ball player's objective in life: "We try to live good, clean lives, but whether or not we do is for our wives to judge."

Jim Davenport, who played for and managed the San Francisco Giants, was married while still in high school in Siluria, Ala. As a senior, Davenport was caught going to the pool hall instead of class. What happened next to Davenport had to be a great embarrassment. "The principal dragged us back to school and whipped us with a paddle that had holes in it," he recalled. "I'd been married for over a year, and here I was getting a spanking."

Announcer Harry Caray said time became more meaningful to him after being divorced: "I never realized how short a month is until I started paying alimony."

Don Larsen's wife filed for divorce on the very day that he pitched a perfect game for the Yankees in the World Series.

Sex and the Baseball Player

Casey Stengel always had something to say about everything, so it should come as no surprise that the legendary manager would offer these comments about baseball and sex: "You gotta learn that if you don't get it by midnight, chances are you ain't gonna get it. And if you do, it ain't worth it."

Casey's "midnight" may have been an indirect reference to a team curfew. Not all teams have a curfew, but Chuck Tanner's Pittsburgh Pirates did. Pitcher Bob Veale explained how it affected him: "Chuck Tanner used to have a bed check just for me every night. No problem. My bed was always there."

Outfielder Ken Griffey was chosen to do a public service announcement on television for family planning. On the same day that Griffey's ad debuted on TV, he was served with a paternity suit.

Baseball players make a great deal of money, so they often receive mail from the outside world informing them of "great deals" to be made with that money. After Dave Winfield signed a multimillion-dollar contract with the Yankees, he received a letter from a California lady who wanted him to invest in her business. The lady described that business as "a house of ill repute."

Bobby Grich of the Angels always enjoys the female fans at the ball park, but sometimes there are letdowns. "I spent 15 years honing my baseball skills, $110 at a tanning salon and $35 having my hair styled," he said. "Then I got benched on National Secretaries Day. There is no justice."

Through the years, the Angels' Anaheim Stadium has been one of baseball's better locations for girl watching. Rod Carew played with the Angels for seven seasons, so he certainly knows the score. "The way they dress here, your head is always in the stands," he said. "All those bikinis—your eyes get tired."

Kirk Gibson of the Detroit Tigers once supplied his own distraction. His date for the game was actress Morgan Fairchild. After striking out at the plate, Gibson actually had the gall to blame his date: "I kept looking at her instead of the ball."

When there's a choice to be made in baseball, it's an easy one—at least for Reggie Jackson: "I don't even enjoy sex anymore. I go out with my girl and just sit there. She says, 'Don't you want to touch me?' and I answer, 'No, I just want some hits.' "

The Fairer Sex Strikes Back

Professional baseball has seen female owners, female umpires and female sportswriters. But 17-year-old Jackie Mitchell might go down in history as the most incredible female in the history of baseball.

In 1931, Joe Engel, owner of the minor league Chattanooga Lookouts, signed lefthanded pitcher Jackie Mitchell to a regular team contract for the upcoming season. Although Jackie was signed for the entire 1931 Southern Association season, her debut would come in an exhibition game against the Yankees on April 2.

In the top of the first inning, the first two Yankees got on base. Lookouts Manager Bert Niehoff yanked his starter and called in the young lefthander to face New York's No. 3 batter, Babe Ruth.

The Bambino would go on to bat .373 that season with 46 home runs and 163 runs batted in, but on this particular day, Jackie Mitchell got the best of him. On a 2-2 count, Jackie's sidearm curveball fooled the Babe, who admired it for a called strike three. Ruth reacted with mock anger as he made his way back to the visiting dugout. A grinning Lou Gehrig couldn't hide his smile as he passed the Babe on his way to the plate.

Gehrig would hit .341 with 46 homers and 184 RBIs that season—but that was against American League pitching. On this day he, too, would have to face Chattanooga's 17-year-old distaff lefty curveballer. Jackie made it two in a row as the Iron Horse went down swinging.

Tony Lazzeri was next and salvaged a minor victory for "malekind" by drawing a base on balls. That was all for Mitchell, who was promptly taken out by the Lookouts' manager.

The Yankees clubbed Chattanooga, 14-4, but Jackie Mitchell, whose contract was later disallowed by Commissioner Kenesaw Mountain Landis, will always be remembered as the girl who struck out Babe Ruth and Lou Gehrig.

Baseball Can Be Hazardous To Your Health

(Survival of the Fittest)

"I'll never be considered one of the all-time greats, but I'm one of the all-time survivors."—Jim Kaat, pitcher.

It is a medical miracle that Pete Reiser survived as long as he did in the major leagues (1940-52). Twice in his career, Reiser was beaned. Once he broke a bone in his right elbow, so he learned to throw left-handed. About a dozen times Pistol Pete had to be carried from the field, later regaining consciousness in the clubhouse or a hospital. Reiser was given last rites on one occasion. He repeatedly broke his collarbone, dislocated his shoulder or suffered concussions by crashing into outfield walls. And Pistol Pete once underwent surgery for a blood clot on his brain.

Many of today's players have also survived despite medical maladies that would test the courage of the most intrepid of individuals.

There Are Pitching Woes . . .

Relief pitcher Ray Fontenot of the Chicago Cubs suffered bruised ribs when he fell on his way to answering the bullpen telephone.

Minnesota Twins relief pitcher Doug Corbett broke his toe running to that nasty phone.

The Texas Rangers' Charlie Hough broke the little finger on his pitching hand when he shook hands with a friend.

While a member of the Houston Astros, knuckleball pitcher Joe Niekro burned his fingers by taking a pan out of a decidedly un-friendly oven.

Cubs pitcher Ron Meridith was once hit in the face by the backswing of teammate Dick Ruthven, who was hitting fungoes. Infielder Dave Owen ran for the trainer but hit his head on the dugout roof and was

knocked unconscious. Meridith was taken to the hospital with a concussion. Who knows what happened to Owen?

The Baltimore Orioles' Jim Palmer pinched a nerve in his neck—by looking over at first base.

. . . And Batting Blows

Outfielder Kirk Gibson of the Detroit Tigers injured his collarbone by hitting himself with a bat.

Tigers first baseman Mike Laga broke his wrist when he swung his bat and missed.

The Tigers' Tom Brookens hit a home run and then pulled a hamstring muscle in his trot around the bases.

Pedro Guerrero of the Los Angeles Dodgers strained his back hitting a home run.

Dodgers second baseman Steve Sax didn't even have to swing. He reinjured a previous knee injury when he took a pitch.

Dave Kingman of the Oakland A's had to miss 11 games because he injured his knee when he turned in the batter's box to argue with the umpire.

Watch Out for Animals

Pitcher Greg Minton of the San Francisco Giants hammered a nail into his hand—while shoeing a horse—and was out of action for 10 days.

The San Diego Padres' Goose Gossage cut his finger while eating a lobster.

Bob Ojeda of the Boston Red Sox blamed his poor pitching performance on a bee that stung him during the national anthem.

Nolan Ryan of the Astros had to get rabies shots because he was bitten by a baby coyote.

Even Non-Players Suffer

Dodgers third-base coach Joe Amalfitano broke his thumb when he congratulated Steve Sax for hitting a home run.

Bill Sellers of Concordia College's Department of Exercise Science was invited to spring training by the Montreal Expos to serve as a conditioning coach. Sellers was showing the Expos how to avoid pulled muscles by stretching properly when he suffered a pulled muscle.

Terry Harper of the Atlanta Braves dislocated his shoulder while standing at home plate, waving in a teammate from third base.

Braves coach Russ Nixon took the opposite tack and pulled a calf muscle while trying to hold up a runner at third base.

The Slightest Little Thing

Jerry Hairston of the Chicago White Sox pulled a muscle in his neck when he reached up to put a baseball cap on his head.

Bruce Benedict of the Braves had to leave a game when he pulled a muscle in his neck by putting on his catcher's mitt.

New York Yankees outfielder Henry Cotto was disabled because he punctured his eardrum with a cotton swab.

Jose Cardenal couldn't play one opening day for the Cubs because his eyelid was stuck shut.

San Francisco's Chris Brown once missed five games because of an injury. Brown's explanation caused some raised eyebrows: "Slept on my eye wrong."

From Boots to Bowling and Beyond

Boston's Wade Boggs suffered bruised ribs while trying to take off his cowboy boots. A few days later he reinjured his ribs. How? By breathing.

Yankees Manager Billy Martin appeared with a broken arm after a fight with pitcher Ed Whitson. Martin, however, claimed he broke his arm while bowling.

Pitcher Ernie Camacho of the Cleveland Indians complained of a sore arm. Earlier that day he had been required to autograph 100 pictures.

Catcher Marc Hill of the White Sox was burned on the face when teammate Dennis Lamp set his beard on fire while lighting a cigarette.

Home Is Where the Hurt Is

Indians pitcher Jamie Easterly pulled a groin muscle while watching television; he crossed his legs.

The Dodgers' Ken Landreaux sprained his knee getting up from a sofa.

Tigers relief pitcher Willie Hernandez fell down the stairs at his home and injured his ribs. He fell down a second time and injured his back.

Not to be outdone, Goose Gossage of the Padres injured his back when he sneezed. He had to be kept out of action for five days.

While pitching for the California Angels, Don Aase went Goose one step better and separated cartilage in his rib cage with a sneeze.

Tito Landrum of the St. Louis Cardinals strained a back muscle when he stood up from the dinner table, while White Sox pitcher Britt Burns picked a different room in which to pull a neck muscle—he was getting out of bed.

Dodgers pitcher Orel Hershiser pulled a back muscle in spring training by picking up his 1-year-old son.

Steve Trout of the Cubs couldn't pitch because he bruised his left shoulder when he fell off his bicycle.

Gorman Thomas of the Milwaukee Brewers injured his back while getting out of a taxi.

Another vehicular victim, outfielder Gary Pettis of the Angels, strained a muscle in his shoulder while adjusting his car seat.

And socks can be as deadly as sneezes. The Yankees' Ed Whitson injured his back by taking his socks off, and Braves infielder Randy Johnson sprained his thumb in spring training while pulling off a sock.

What's Up, Doc?

Not all physical problems in baseball are the responsibility of the patient. Doctors can make mistakes. After all, almost 50 percent of all doctors finished in the bottom half of their class.

1985 was a year that the Rangers' team physician, B.J. Mycoskie, won't soon forget. Dr. Mycoskie gave Yankees Manager Billy Martin an injection for back spasms—and punctured his lung. Mycoskie then gave Kansas City Royals center fielder Willie Wilson a penicillin injection for a cold. Wilson suffered an allergic reaction to the shot and was unable to play for 2½ weeks.

Indians Manager Pat Corrales came to the defense of Dr. Mycoskie, whom he knew from his days as manager of the Rangers. "He's a good doctor," Corrales said. "He just had a bad year."

Take Two Aspirin and. . .

Angels pitcher Bruce Kison was not one to go to the medical profes-

sion for advice. "The only doctors that can tell me how I'm doing now," he said, "are Dr. Rice, Dr. Murray and Dr. Luzinski."

Reggie Jackson is another player who was not in a hurry to go to a doctor. Reggie's reason: "I don't need a physical. My problem is between my ears."

Infielder Aurelio Rodriguez also liked to diagnose his own injuries. As a member of the Padres he collided with Bill North of the Giants. Rodriguez explained how he knew something was broken: "I reached for my nose here and found it over there."

On the other hand, Cleveland's Jamie Easterly was only too happy to heed his doctor's advice. The pitcher returned from being treated for a rash and reported: "The doctor told me I can't run for the rest of the season. And I can drink only Chivas Regal."

Many of baseball's most serious injuries are suffered by pitchers. Several theories have been developed to explain why pitchers have so much difficulty. Perhaps Yogi Berra said it best when he commented on the disability of lefthander Shane Rawley: "Getting hurt hurt him."

Twins outfielder Mickey Hatcher has had more than his share of misfortune. Said Mickey: "I wake up in the morning, take one look in the mirror and immediately start limping."

Most athletes are expected to play with some degree of pain. The Philadelphia Phillies' Mike Schmidt had a cracked rib but shook it off: "It feels good unless I breathe, sneeze, cough or bend over."

Harvey Kuenn, who managed the 1982 pennant-winning Brewers, pointed out that a physical disability can turn out to be a plus. Kuenn referred to his artificial right leg: "Greatest thing that ever happened to me. Now I get all the choice parking places." It also proved to be an advantage on the field: "My relievers like it when I go out to the mound to take a starter out because they have so much extra time to warm up."

New York newspaper columnist Dick Young has poked fun at players who often were sidelined with injuries. For instance: "The Braves' Bob Horner is on the disabled list more often than eggs are on a grocery list." And about Dave Kingman: "His home address is: Disabled List, U.S.A."

If You Can't Believe Your Doctor. . .

Tigers Manager Sparky Anderson is not one to say that he distrusts the entire medical profession. It's just that he prefers the hometown doc. When Kirk Gibson was injured in early 1986 in Boston, the diagnosis was a badly sprained ankle. Gibson then was flown back to Detroit for another examination. Sparky explained: "They'll re-X-ray a lot of things. There are a lot of things that can look a lot different two days later. They might have trick X-rays in Boston."

Paul Owens, former Phillies manager, is smart enough to see the funny side of baseball.

Get Smart

"I tell every kid I talk to that they should make sure they get a college education before signing a pro contract. You don't have to know anything to get a college degree, but if you've got one, people think you're intelligent."—Calvin Griffith, former Minnesota Twins owner.

Collegiate Candor

Traditional wisdom has ball players signing contracts right out of high school in order to take full advantage of minor league experience. Higher education has not exactly been a prerequisite for a high batting average.

Today, more players are using college as their minor league system. But that's not to say they're planning careers as brain surgeons—nor that the brains involved are all that much smarter!

Mike Flanagan, pitcher, Baltimore Orioles and University of Massachusetts:
"In my sophomore year there, I had more complete games than credits."

Tim Laudner, catcher, Twins and University of Missouri:
"I majored in eligibility."

Mike Pagliarulo, third baseman, New York Yankees and University of Miami (Fla.):
"I didn't know it was a grand slam until I rounded third and saw three people waiting for me at home plate."

English 101

Paul Owens, manager/general manager, Philadelphia Phillies:
"You can lead a horse to water, but you can't stick his head in it."

"I'm not one of those front-office types who hides behind their ivory towers."

Jim Morrison, infielder, Pittsburgh Pirates (about the team's owner offering to sell):
"I don't think Pittsburgh people appreciate baseball. I'm glad to see Dan Galbreath take the bull by the reins."

Johnny Logan, shortstop, Milwaukee Braves:
   "I know the name, but I can't replace the face."

Jesse Orosco, pitcher, New York Mets (about the awesome potential of teammate Darryl Strawberry):
   "He's got all the utilities."

Gary Carter, catcher, Montreal Expos (about the team's new manager, who stepped down from the front office during the 1981 season):
   "Jim Fanning lit a torch under our fire."

Dale Murphy, outfielder, Atlanta Braves:

"I'm a natural lefthander, but I bat and throw right-handed because that's the way I learned. But I eat left and drink left and write left. I'm amphibious."

Charlie Kerfeld, pitcher, Houston Astros:
   "We're a team of destination."

Bob Stanley, pitcher, Boston Red Sox (about a local newspaper story that upset him):
   "I'm going to cancel my prescription."

Dave Tomlin, pitcher, Expos (about a Pittsburgh outfielder shying away from the outfield wall):
   "He heard footprints."

English 102

Pitcher Mike Smith, who came up through the Cincinnati Reds' organization and was traded to the Expos after the 1986 season, has been known to make statements that would make Yogi Berra proud.

(Ordering a salad from a waitress):
   "Make sure you put on a bunch of those neutrons."

(Checking out of a hotel):
"I'm here to pay my accidentals."

(On why he bought a new coat):
"Because it has good installation."

Spanish 101

Paul Owens, Phillies (at a Mexican restaurant):
"Take good care of us, Jose. We're Numero One-o."

Clay Carroll, pitcher, Reds (to teammate Pedro Borbon):
"Hey, Pedro, how do you say 'adios' in Spanish?"

Baseball: It's a Brain Drain

Lee Mazzilli, outfielder, Mets:
"This is a head game. And when you have your head screwed on right, it makes it easier."

Bill Caudill, pitcher, Seattle Mariners:
"I have a strong arm. And with a little brains, I can go a long way."

Scott McGregor, pitcher, Orioles:
"I don't want to think too much because I get confused. I don't want to think. . . . I just want to pitch."

Neil Allen, pitcher, Chicago White Sox:
"I let my mind drift. I can be lackadaisical. . . . It's no big secret that Neil Allen is no brain surgeon."

Britt Burns, pitcher, White Sox:
"I think too much on the mound sometimes, and I get brain cramps."

Jim Lonborg, pitcher, Red Sox (when asked if baseball is more mental than physical):
"If it was, I'd be soaking my head in ice, not my arm."

Roy Smalley, infielder, Twins (about teammate Mickey Hatcher):
"He's the first guy ever to make the majors on one brain cell."

Rick Monday, outfielder, Los Angeles Dodgers (about San Francisco's Mike Ivie):
"A $40 million airport—with a $30 million control tower."

Doug Rader, manager, Texas Rangers:
"This won't be another 'Ball Four.' It's going to be a family book. I'm just writing down a lot of things that go through my mind, so there will probably be a lot of blank pages."

Where Did These Guys Matriculate?

Kelly Paris, infielder, Cardinals (when told he would playing in Venezuela in the winter):
"Where'd you get that idea? That's not true. I'm playing in Maracaibo."

Roy Smalley, Twins:
"When you have been through what I've been through, you have to come to grips with your own culpability."

John Kruk, outfielder, San Diego Padres (about his first visit to Chicago and seeing Lake Michigan):
"What ocean is that?"

(Later): "Oh, I know it's Lake Michigan now. Originally I thought it was the Mediterranean."

Tony Gwynn, outfielder, Padres (after San Diego lost the first two games of the 1984 National League Championship Series):
"There's no tomorrow if we don't win tomorrow."

Probing Questions

Jerry Willard, a catcher for the Cleveland Indians, is no sponge when it comes to absorbing new information. Willard mulls over the facts and asks pertinent questions before committing the information to memory.

(When told that the Twins won a doubleheader):
"Who won the first game?"

(When told by the trainer that he should gargle with lukewarm water):
"Where do you go to buy that stuff?"

Baseball Double-Talk (and Triple-Talk)

Mark Bradley, outfielder, Mets:
"We can do what we can do. All we have to do is do what we can do."

Reggie Jackson, outfielder, California Angels (about Manager Gene Mauch):
"When a guy plays you to the point that you think you should be playing more, then something is happening right."

Ernie Banks, infielder, Chicago Cubs (about baseball):
"You know why it's the most unique game in the world? Because it ameliorates the classic polarization between self-motivated individuals and collective ideology."

Peter Bavasi, president, Indians (about White Sox Manager Tony LaRussa):
"LaRussa is a very bright man. He's a lawyer in the off-season, although that doesn't necessarily mean he's smart."

The Final Word(s)

Jim Bouton, former major league pitcher (about Seattle Pilots Manager Joe Schultz):
"Joe Schultz would have been a better manager if he understood

more. Of course, if he understood more, he might not have been a manager."

Don Zimmer, coach, Cubs (when asked, upon regaining consciousness from a fall, who was President before Ronald Reagan):
"I don't know. I didn't know before I fell, either."

Elliott Maddox, outfielder, Mets:
"I have an off-season vocabulary and a during-the-season vocabulary. I guess you could say I'm bilingual."

W.P. Kinsella, novelist (when asked if he knew any literate baseball players):
"Tom Seaver is the only one who comes to mind. But I do know that Steve Boros reads."

Graig Nettles, third baseman, Yankees (about teammate Tommy John):
"Ask him the time, and he'll tell you how to build a watch."

Cal McLish, scout, Milwaukee Brewers:
"The definition of a smart player is someone who can't play."

Yesterday's Heroes

(How Quickly We Forget)

"I never heard of Gehrig until I came here. And I always thought Babe Ruth was a cartoon character. I really did."
—Don Mattingly, first baseman, New York Yankees.

Babe and Lou Who?

In 1981, rookie infielder Andre Robertson of the New York Yankees was issued uniform number 55. Andre felt like a giant to be a Yankee, but he was somewhat less than thrilled about his new number. "Gee, 55 is an awfully high number, especially for an infielder," he said. "Don't you have something lower? I've been looking around, and I've noticed no one is wearing numbers 3 or 4."

Former relief pitcher Tug McGraw, somewhat of a folk hero himself, names Babe Ruth as one of the three men he most admires. That's quite a compliment for the Babe, who finishes second only to Elvis Presley and just ahead of Benjamin Franklin.

The Babe, considered by many to be the greatest baseball player in history, has his Yankee locker on display at the Hall of Fame in Cooperstown, N.Y., where it can be admired by thousands of fans. Like Babe Ruth, Willie Mays also is considered by many to be the greatest player in baseball history. Mays spent more than two decades with the New York and San Francisco Giants, and he still has a locker in the Giants' clubhouse in San Francisco. Willie's locker also is put to use—the Giants' batting-practice pitchers change their clothes there.

No Respect

Before the 1985 Cotton Bowl game in Dallas, Auburn football star Bo Jackson, that year's Heisman Trophy winner, was asked if he would consider giving up football to play for the Texas Rangers. Bo's response: "Who are the Texas Rangers?"

After hitting a particularly long home run, New York Mets outfielder Darryl Strawberry was asked if he thought the ball would have gone out of the Polo Grounds. Darryl's response: "What is the Polo Grounds?"

The University of Minnesota's Dave Winfield was the No. 1 draft choice of the San Diego Padres on June 5, 1973. Winfield, who went straight from college to the major leagues, was asked if he was happy that the Padres had drafted him. Winfield's response: "I'd never heard of them, and that's the truth."

After pitching for six seasons in the Mexican League, Salome Barojas joined the Chicago White Sox in 1982. While pitching in relief against the Yankees, Barojas was asked if he knew how to pitch against slugger Dave Winfield. Salome's response: "Who is this Winfield? I don't know any of the players on the team."

Many youngsters play baseball at Don Sutton Park in Molino, Fla., the hometown of Don Sutton's parents. When Sutton won his 300th game for the California Angels in 1986, 7-year-old Zachary Reigel was asked about Sutton's achievement. Zachary's response: "I thought he was somebody that died a long time ago."

Admiration Society

Tom Seaver, a Mets pitcher for 10½ years before being traded to the Cincinnati Reds, was traded back to New York before the 1983 season. Young relief pitcher Doug Sisk was thrilled to have the Mets' No. 1 hero back in New York. But he did have one problem concerning the return of a legend. "I don't know whether to call him 'Sir' or 'Mister,' " he said.

Pete Rose is one of the most famous men ever to have played baseball. Mike Schmidt, the Philadelphia Phillies' great third baseman, admires his former teammate. "Pete Rose is the most likable arrogant person I've ever met," he said.

Baseball's all-time strikeout king, righthander Nolan Ryan of the Houston Astros, is another big fan of Pete Rose. "Pete's one of the best ever to play the game," Ryan said. "The only difference I can see between now and when I first faced him 14 years ago is that his hair is longer and he has gotten a little uglier."

I'm Not Sure I Got That Name

Perennial All-Star third baseman George Brett batted .390 in 1980 and led the Kansas City Royals to the World Series. But when George Brett's name was the puzzle on television's popular "Wheel of Fortune" game show, not one of three contestants could figure out who he was until only one letter was missing:

GE_RGE BRETT

On April 29, 1986, Roger Clemens of the Boston Red Sox set a major league record by striking out 20 Seattle Mariners. When Bob Gibson was asked about young Clemens' performance, the Hall of Fame pitcher expressed his surprise: "Amazing! I'm not even sure who Roger Clemens is."

Maybe Gibson just wanted to forget. When the Mets drafted Roger Clemens in 1981, Gibson was the club's pitching coach. Gibson scouted the righthander and was not impressed, so when Clemens demanded $5,000 more than the Mets were offering him to sign, the Mets let the young prospect return to college. Five years later, when Clemens led Boston to the World Series against New York, the Mets could only dream about Clemens being in the same starting rotation as Dwight Gooden, Ron Darling and Bob Ojeda.

You Have To Take The Bitter With . . . Executive Sweets

Out of executive suites come many executive sweets—from the commissioner of baseball all the way down to the lowest mailroom clerk.

Starting at the Top

No one ever accused baseball executives of being among the Einsteins of America. No SAT scores are required to produce baseball scores. And even baseball's highest of the high shuns the accusation of brilliance.

Peter Ueberroth, commissioner:
> "I'm not very smart. I think I can prove that. Who would accept a job with Marge Schott's dog, Ted Turner and George Steinbrenner as your boss?"

When Bowie Kuhn was ousted as commissioner, he knew that the search committee would try to replace him with the impossible.

Bowie Kuhn:
> "You know, they're probably looking for a non-existent person. But I'm positive they'll find such a person."

Edward Bennett Williams, owner, Baltimore Orioles:
> "They're looking for someone who is knowledgeable about the game, knowledgeable about the economic aspects of the industry, who has strong leadership, unquestioned integrity, great ability . . . industrious, honest, able. If we find that sort of fellow, I want to run him for President."

After having to deal with countries all over the world in his position as president of the Los Angeles Olympic Organizing Committee, the new commissioner was quite pleased to have a new position, this one smaller in scope. Said Ueberroth: "I've been vilified in 20 languages. It'll be nice to be reduced to one."

The new commissioner also was pleased when A. Bartlett Giamatti, Yale's president, was named president of the National League. Already manning that post in the American League was another man whose name was preceded by the title "Dr."—Bobby Brown, a cardiologist. Said Ueberroth: "Now that we have a doctor as president of both leagues, maybe they can solve the ills of the game."

Ueberroth was honored as Time magazine's Man of the Year. Baseball's newest top gun found out about the prestigious award by neither telephone nor telegram, though—he was notified when he dropped by the local 7-Eleven store and saw his picture on the cover.

Nothing Comes Between Him and His Calvins

Until recent years, major league baseball on the local level was usually run by real baseball people who grew up in the game of baseball, many of them in baseball families. And most of them made their livelihood solely from the national pastime.

Calvin R. Griffith was exactly this kind of baseball executive and club owner. As a boy, Calvin was adopted by his uncle, Clark Griffith, who had won 240 games as a big-league pitcher and later was inducted into the Hall of Fame.

Because Clark Griffith was the owner of the Washington Senators, young Calvin learned the baseball trade by starting at the bottom, first serving as the team batboy, and working his way up. He became the owner and president of the team when the senior Griffith died in 1955.

The Senators moved to Minnesota for the 1961 season and became the Minnesota Twins. The Twins won the American League pennant in 1965 and captured the first two A.L. West titles in 1969-70. The team came upon hard times in the 1980s, however, and Griffith was forced to sell. The former owner, president and chairman of the board of the Senators and Twins is still involved with the team today as a consultant.

The legacy of Calvin R. Griffith will always live, and so will his "outa-sight" insights into the game of baseball.

(About advertising):
> "I think that if you have a good product, you don't need to advertise it. And if you have a lousy product, it isn't any use to advertise it."

(About players' salaries):
> "Money does nothin' but ruin ball players."

(About pitcher Terry Felton's spring training):
> "Terry Felton isn't going north until he gets a haircut, a shave and a changeup."

(About rookie outfielder Jim Eisenreich):
> "I saw that kid play at Wisconsin Rapids last year. I knew immediately he was *doomed* to become an All-Star center fielder."

(About the future):
> "I can't tell you exactly what I intend to do. But I can tell you one thing; it won't be anything rational."

(About life after selling the Twins):
> "Honestly, I'm having a great deal of fun. Hey, I go to the supermarket and everyone stops to talk to me. When I owned the team, no one would talk to me."

Calvins may not fade, but they have been known to rub off, especially on one's offspring. Consider these words from Calvin's son, Clark Griffith:
> "Before the season, we took a survey of the fans and found out they want to see home runs more than anything else. So we went out to build a pitching staff to oblige them."

The Mouth of the South

In contrast to Calvin Griffith and baseball's old regime of executives, today's young Turks (some insensitive individuals would add the letters "eys" to that moniker!) have ushered in the flamboyant style of a new regime. One such example is Ted Turner, global pacifist, occasional working nudist (he once conducted an executive meeting in the nude, wearing only a cigar) and owner of the Atlanta Braves.

R.E. (Ted) Turner purchased
the Braves on January 14, 1976,
and the game of baseball has not
been the same since. Turner
thinks big and acts big, and
through his television network,
the Braves became known as
"America's Team."

Ted is not only a television mag-
nate and the inspiration for Ash-
ley Dashley III, owner of TV station K-Bloom in the Bloom
County comic strip, but he's also
a sportsman. He was Yachtsman
of the Year four times. He created the Goodwill Games. He owns
the Atlanta Hawks in the National Basketball Association.
And he even appointed himself
manager of the Braves, replacing
Dave Bristol for one game in 1977 before N.L. President Chub Feeney
stepped in to protect the integrity of the game.

Ted Turner also likes to talk . . . and talk . . . and talk.

(About Commissioner Bowie Kuhn):
> "I went into the clubhouse and asked them (the players) if any-
> body thought Bowie Kuhn was doing a good job. I said, 'If you
> think so, raise your hand.' Only one person raised his hand—Ru-
> fino Linares. And he didn't understand the question."

(About winning):
> "What you've got to have in baseball is pitching, speed and
> money."

(About the 1982 baseball season):
> "There are lots of reasons why we can win the West Division,
> including the fact that we don't have any crazies, flakes or drug
> addicts on the team. Our future is so bright, it's unbelievable.
> Almost." (Ted was right—almost. There were no flakes or cra-
> zies on that team, unless you consider such players as Al Hra-
> bosky, Pascual Perez, Claudell Washington and Bob Walk some-

thing other than run-of-the-mill, everyday guys. But the Braves did win the N.L. West that year.)

(About the 1982 pennant race):
"The only thing I worry about is clinching the division too early. I like making money."

(About winning the N.L. West title in 1982):
"Dynasty! Dynasty! Dynasty!"

(About Manager Bobby Cox):
"I think he's a terrific manager and a terrific person, but sometimes you have to make a change."

(About Manager Eddie Haas):
"Considering the fact we've had pitching problems and that we haven't scored a lot of runs in key situations, we think Eddie Haas has done a fine job."

(About the Soviet Union's boycott of the 1984 Olympics):
"It's like having a World Series and the American League doesn't show up."

(About the Goodwill Games in Moscow in 1986):
"We're going to be great friends with the Russians. It's going to be a snap to stop the arms race."

(About his own remarks):
"Seems like everything I say comes back to haunt me."

(About his intelligence):
"I may be dumb, but I'm not stupid."

Beware of Executivespeak

Despite the forthrightness of such personalities as Calvin Griffith and Ted Turner, you may think that "no comment" and double-speak are standard fare for most discussions involving baseball executives. Not so. The inhabitants of the front-office chairs have been known to express an opinion or two through the years. For instance:

Ballard Smith, San Diego Padres:
"I don't think we will miss Dave Winfield. He played here eight

years, but we were in last place (actually second division) for
eight years."

Roy Eisenhardt, owner, Oakland A's:
"I don't think Winfield could start in our outfield. There's no
room for Winfield unless we had a 10-man softball team."

"We have to have the players association or we're going to turn
into wrestling."

George Argyros, owner, Seattle Mariners:
"If Tom Paciorek will guarantee his performance, we will guarantee his contract."

"Never in the 100-year history of baseball has a team been com-
petitive in the first 10 years of its existence." (The New York
Mets won the World Series in their eighth season. The Kansas
City Royals won the A.L. West in their eighth season. The Toronto Blue Jays won the A.L. East in their ninth season.)

John McHale, owner, Montreal Expos:
"There is no way an ordinary mortal can evaluate everything Bill
(Spaceman) Lee tells me in a short period. I need time to put it
into the computer."

Tom Monaghan, owner, Detroit Tigers:
"The way free agency has worked out, free agents haven't done
that well, including our 1984 pick, Darrell Evans. He batted only
.232 and cost us $750,000 a year. What are we going to do with
him? We've got some people in the farm system who can do
better than that." (Fortunately for Evans, the Tigers decided to
let him finish the season in 1985, despite having "better" players
in the farm system. Darrell hit 40 home runs to lead the major
leagues.)

Al Rosen, San Francisco Giants (about pitcher Mark Grant):
"A million-dollar arm and a 10-cent brain."

Lou Gorman, Boston Red Sox (about Roger Clemens' record-setting
20 strikeouts in a 1986 game):
"If he keeps up those kinds of performances, he could end up
being an attraction."

Phyllis K. Merhige, A.L. office (when asked why Royals reliever Dan Quisenberry was not named Player of the Week after posting four saves and one victory in five scoreless outings):
>"I know, but he only pitched 7⅓ innings."

Jay Horwitz, Mets:
>"Kingman had one game-winner but would have had two more except that the Mets lost the games."

>"Bob Bailor got beaned in the wrist."

Eddie Einhorn, owner, Chicago White Sox:
>"Very few of our players understood the whole situation. We didn't always know everything, either. I had to call Sports Phone."

>"Show me a team in last place, and I'll show you a death watch."

Marge Schott, owner, Cincinnati Reds:
>"I wish they'd give me a scorecard with pictures because I still get everybody mixed up."

>(On Mother's Day): "Boys, if you love your mother, you will win this one."

Frank Cashen, Mets:
>"We in management are united by our problems and divided by our solutions."

Dallas Green, Philadelphia Phillies:
>"Maybe I acted a little bit like a fool, but that is part of baseball."

>(About training with bikes and weights): "You can't ride a bike between second and third base, and you can't lift your batting average with a set of weights."

Peter Bavasi, Blue Jays:
>"I was thinking about going up and watching the team play tonight, but I decided, 'Why torture myself?'"

Ken (Hawk) Harrelson, White Sox:
>"If there has been a mistake made here, it's that I've been too

honest with everybody. I'm going to correct that in the future."

Buzzie Bavasi, California Angels:
"Gene Autry and I supported the (Olympic) Games from the start and still do. I like the idea of having it here—every 52 years."

"Years and years ago, the National League met one time and took a vote to change the per capita shares. We did it to help one club. The vote was 11 to one. The one guy we voted to help was the one guy who voted against it."

"You can never have too much talent. Even the 1927 Yankees didn't win every year."

"Right now I'm expecting him (outfielder Ellis Valentine) to do what he did for the Mets last year, which was very little. If he does that, I won't be disappointed."

Bill Veeck, owner, White Sox:
"I was in the game for love. After all, where else can an old-timer like me with one leg, who can't hear or see, live like a king while doing the only thing I wanted to do?"

"Baseball is the only orderly thing in a very unorderly world. If you get three strikes, even Edward Bennett Williams can't get you off."

Jerry Reinsdorf, owner, White Sox:
"The idea is nonsensical, so I guess it will happen."

George Steinbrenner, owner, New York Yankees:
"What has happened is that all your life you operated businesses in such a way that you could one day afford to buy a baseball team. And then you buy the team and forget all the business practices that enabled you to buy it."

Ellis Clary, White Sox (on why he resigned from the Twins to scout for the White Sox):
"Every 40 years I change jobs."

Harry Dalton, Milwaukee Brewers:
"You can tell it's been a bad year when the highlight of the

Brewer highlight film is Brewer Peanut Butter."

Bebe de Roulet, Mets:
"Can't we wash the old baseballs and use them again?"

Sam Meason, Texas Rangers:
"We can market the team like a tube of toothpaste. Winning and losing has no bearing on attendance." (The Rangers lost $11 million in the two years in which Meason served as their executive vice president.)

Andy Dolich, A's:
"We've been considering numerous promotional concepts. I think it might be time to reach out to the gays."

Charlie Finley, owner, A's:
"Over the years, a lot of people have talked about buying the Oakland A's, but all they had were big hats and no cattle."

"I'd like to hire Bowie Kuhn so I could have the pleasure of firing the clown the very next day."

(On the telephone to Manager Hank Bauer during a game): "I noticed when you went out to the mound, you had grass stains on the seat of your pants. That's not a good example to set for your players."

Bauer: "Those weren't grass stains, Charlie. That was mistletoe."

Baseball and Politics—Strange Bedfellows

President Ronald Reagan (to Los Angeles Dodgers Manager Tom Lasorda):

"If your team is doing half as well as I am, you'll win the World Series."

President Jimmy Carter:

"I've been trying to write a book and listen to the Braves' games at the same time. The Braves are delaying the completion of my book."

Canadian Prime Minister Pierre Trudeau:

"Do you have any idea how difficult it is being prime minister of a country in which (Expos catcher) Gary Carter could be elected tomorrow?"

Biting the Hand That Feeds You

Marvin Miller, executive director of the Major League Players Asso-

ciation (about major league owners):

    "This is the worst damn dictatorship since Nazi Germany."

Keith Moreland, outfielder, Chicago Cubs:

    "It's amazing. The owners claim they are going to put their foot down. Then they turn around and wrap their mouths around it."

Marvin Davis (about Charlie Finley, from whom he attempted to buy the A's in 1977):

    "He's an old reprobate. No self-respecting fish would be wrapped in the comment of Charlie Finley."

Chuck Connors, baseball player-turned-actor (about Brooklyn Dodgers Owner Branch Rickey, his onetime boss):

    "Rickey had both money and players. He just didn't like to see the two of them mix."

Bob Drury, sportswriter, in Sport magazine (about Donald Fehr, executive director of the players association):

    "Remember how Marvin Miller terrorized the lords of baseball? These days, the owners have nothing to fear but Fehr himself."

Kirk Gibson, free-agent outfielder (about possibly re-signing with the Tigers):

    "For me to sign a three-year contract and then shake hands with Bill Lajoie or Jim Campbell, I think I would vomit." (Shortly thereafter, Kirk agreed to a multimillion-dollar, three-year contract with Detroit.)

Tim Sullivan, Cincinnati Enquirer (about Reds President Dick Wagner):

    "He was always available—for a 'no comment.' "

Dave Concepcion, Reds shortstop (about Mrs. Dick Wagner's broken wrist):

    "Gloria really broke her wrist trying to get Wagner's wallet out of his pocket."

Mike Downey, sportswriter, in The Sporting News (about Reds Owner Marge Schott's dog):

    "Word out of Cincinnati is that Schottzie the St. Bernard will be a guest on 'Late Night With David Letterman' next week to do Stupid Owner Tricks."

Reggie Jackson, outfielder, Angels:
"I'd like to be a minority owner—no pun intended—after I retire."

Baseball Management's Believe It or Not

Yankees executive Cedric Tallis was once sent to Japan on a scouting
expedition. His mission was to scout scoreboards.

Blue Jays General Manager Pat Gillick signed the following players to
baseball contracts at various stages of his career: Danny Ainge, Jay
Schroeder, Bob Bourne and Clark Gillies. Ainge now plays for the
Boston Celtics, Schroeder for the Washington Redskins and Bourne
and Gillies in the National Hockey League.

Mets Vice President Lou Gorman thought his club needed a lefthanded pitcher, so he talked to the Royals about the possibility of acquir-
ing Mike Armstrong. Armstrong is righthanded.

The Rangers once hired Jim Medick as the team's new marketing
director, even though he once admitted that he had never heard of
Bill Veeck. Medick decided to do away with Bat Day, Ball Day and
Cap Day. Instead, he planned to institute jalapeno-eating contests.

In 1972, the Rangers made their debut in the A.L. standings, replacing
the Washington Senators. One decade later, however, the Senators
were still programmed into the computer of the Oakland A's message
board.

Kerplunk Into a Slump

"Slump? I ain't in no slump. I just ain't hitting."—Yogi Berra, catcher, New York Yankees.

A Slump Is a Slump Is a Slump

Steve Kemp, outfielder, Pittsburgh Pirates:
"The only people in the U.S. who had a worse night than me died."

Keith Hernandez, first baseman, New York Mets:
"I'm in as deep a slump as I can be. I'm in a dark forest. No sun. No foliage. Can't tell where west, east, north or south is."

Terry Kennedy, catcher, San Diego Padres:
"Most slumps are like the common cold. They last two weeks, no matter what you do."

Bo Jackson, outfielder, Memphis Chicks (Southern):
"Life is full of slumps. You come out of it. It's not like the bubonic plague or something."

Fran Healy, announcer, Mets:
"When you are in a slump and you have all that stuff in your mind, medically speaking, you need a mental enema."

Enos Cabell, infielder, Detroit Tigers:
"Nobody in the American League East can afford a slump or they'll end up in Yugoslavia."

Mickey Hatcher, outfielder, Minnesota Twins (after striking out):
"He (the pitcher) caught me at a good time. I was 1-for-21 at the time. If I'd been 2-for-21, I'd have gotten him."

Paul Zuvella, infielder, Yankees (on his slump):
"By trying not to think about it, I'm thinking about it."

George Foster, outfielder, Mets:
"There has to be something behind this, other than the fact that I'm not swinging well."

Buck Martinez, catcher, Toronto Blue Jays:
"There were times this year when people looked at the scoreboard and thought my batting average was the temperature."

Bruce Sutter, pitcher, Atlanta Braves (after Atlanta broke a 37-inning scoreless streak):
"We were bound to score a run before the season was over."

Joe Simpson, first baseman, Kansas City Royals (after hitting a triple to end a 0-for-22 slump):
"I'm used to making right turns at first base. Those three quick left-hand turns got to me."

Clint Hurdle, outfielder, Mets (about teammate Howard Johnson, who had just grounded out to second base for the fourth time in one game):
"He's writing a book: 'The Summer of 4 to 3.'"

Odd Cures for Slumps

Tony Gwynn, outfielder, Padres:
"The way we've been doing, we need to face a pitcher with a bad arm, someone with a bad rotator cuff."

Richie Ashburn, outfielder, Philadelphia Phillies:
"To cure a batting slump, I took my bat to bed with me. I wanted to know my bat a little better."

Marty Castillo, catcher, Tigers:
"My bats are in Mexico, undergoing laetrile treatments."

You Can Laugh or You Can. . .

St. Louis Cardinals Manager Whitey Herzog has won his share of championships, including a World Series crown in 1982. But a few of his teams have fared less well. When that happens, Herzog tends to look at the lighter side of the situation.

(About the Cardinals' decision not to show the players' miserable batting averages on the scoreboard for a few home games in 1986):
"Let the fans figure them out. It will give them something to do while we're losing."

(About outfielder Lonnie Smith allegedly striking an umpire):
"One thing I know for sure is that Lonnie didn't punch the guy because if he had swung, he'd have missed, the way we've been hitting."

(About another offensive famine):
"The Clydesdales have been on second base more than our runners."

Words to Slump By

Bob Lemon, manager, Yankees:
"All I know is that the way we are hitting, sick people are getting out of bed and wanting to pitch against us."

Billy Martin, manager, Yankees:
"We could have held batting practice in a hotel lobby that inning and not even broken a lamp."

Champ Summers, outfielder, Padres:
"That was my first bunt base hit in the majors. It was the hardest ball I hit in a month."

Larry Parrish, outfielder, Texas Rangers (about arriving in Baltimore and then losing in a game started by the Orioles' Storm Davis for the 10th consecutive time):
"We were saying last night that Storm Davis probably would have a limousine waiting for us at the airport."

Joe Torre, manager, Braves (about ace pitcher Pascual Perez spending part of the off-season in a Dominican Republic jail):
"Each team has a bad streak. This year we had ours in January."

Ron Kittle, outfielder, Chicago White Sox:
"If I wanted to fail so much, I would've kept taking fifth-grade math."

Ozzie Virgil, catcher, Braves:
"When you're going like we are now, your grandmother can get you out."

Macho Macho Man

"I don't want to get to know the other guys too well. I might like them, and then I might not want to throw at them."—Sal Maglie, pitcher, New York Giants.

Sal Maglie was known as "The Barber" because of the frequent close shaves he gave enemy batters. The great Walter Johnson was another pitcher who struck fear in the hearts of opposing batsmen. Johnson hit a major league-record 206 batters in his career. Don Drysdale holds the modern National League record for hit batsmen with 154. Then there was Early Wynn who, it was said, would even knock down his grandmother.

All of these pitchers developed a macho image with their hard inside pitches. Cincinnati Reds pitcher Ted Davidson, on the other hand, showed some machismo in another manner. After being shot in the chest and stomach by his estranged wife during spring training in 1967, Davidson allowed charges against his wife to be dropped and later pitched for the Reds that season.

In more recent times, there's Cleveland Indians reliever Ernie (Macho) Camacho. The righthander had bone chips removed from his elbow in 1985 and kept them in a jar above his locker.

Seattle Mariners pitcher Edwin Nunez was suspended from the Puerto Rican winter league at the age of 19. That disciplinary action was taken because he threatened the general manager of the team with a gun.

Bob (Whirlybird) Walk of the Pittsburgh Pirates was thrown in jail as a boy because he was caught throwing objects at outfielder Cesar Cedeno from the bleachers at Dodger Stadium.

Minnesota Twins outfielder Gary Ward had his nose broken in five places in 1983 when he was hit by a pitch thrown by Detroit's Dan Petry. When Ward returned to the lineup a mere six days later wearing protective headgear with a plexiglass mask, he went 4-for-4 in his first game.

The Los Angeles Dodgers' Pedro Guerrero was hit in the head by a pitch thrown by the Houston Astros' Nolan Ryan. Pedro's batting helmet was shattered, but he collected it and then took it to Ryan for an autograph.

Dave Winfield, the New York Yankees' 6-foot-6, 220-pound outfielder, was warming up before a 1983 game against the Blue Jays at Toronto's Exhibition Stadium when one of his throws inadvertently struck and killed a sea gull in the outfield. Toronto police officials were not impressed. They hauled Winfield down to the police station and charged him with cruelty to animals. Charges were dropped the next day.

Macho Musings

Dave Parker, outfielder, Reds:
> "Most guys would rather wear a hamburger suit in a lion's den than mess with me."

> "September is panty hose month. No nonsense."

Bobby Valentine, manager, Texas Rangers (about Don Baylor's habit of not even trying to get out of the way of inside pitches):
> "Why should he? That's like a car swerving to avoid a squirrel."

Tom Hausman, pitcher, New York Mets (when asked by non-dog-loving Manager George Bamberger if he had brought his dog to spring training):
> "No! When you were named manager, I shot him."

Brad (the Animal) Lesley, pitcher, Reds:
> "I'm definitely an animal on the mound. . . . I just tune myself out on life and go out there and do it up. . . . They love me in Cincinnati and hate me on the road. They yell vulgar things about my mother and throw stuff at me. It's great."

Tim McCarver, catcher, St. Louis Cardinals (about teammate Bob Gibson):
> "I remember one time going out to the mound to talk with Bob Gibson. He told me to get back behind the plate, that the only thing I knew about pitching was that it was hard to hit."

Gorman Thomas, outfielder, Milwaukee Brewers (about his good looks):
> "Next to Pete Vuckovich, I'm a Rembrandt."

Gene Mauch, manager, California Angels (about Toronto pitcher Dave Stieb):
> "He's good, but I don't think there's anyone in the world who's as good as he *thinks* he is."

Bob Tewksbury, pitcher, Yankees (to Kansas City Royals center fielder Willie Wilson, who had accused him of throwing at him):
> "Why hit you? You're an instant out!"

Pete Vuckovich, pitcher, Brewers:
> "I really hate hitters. They're goofy. They're trying to get me to ruin my career, so I hate them."

Charlie Kerfeld, pitcher, Astros (about his day off):
> "I go out and do a lot of what we call, back home, slam dancing—go out and butt our heads and stuff like that."

Pete Incaviglia, outfielder, Rangers (about what he would do if any pitchers threw at him during his rookie season):
> "Destroy mankind."

Rafael Ramirez, shortstop, Atlanta Braves (explaining why so few players from the Dominican Republic get walked):
> "You have to swing like a man. A walk won't get you off the island."

Tim Flannery, infielder, San Diego Padres (about Manager Dick Wil-

liams):

>"I love playing for Dick, but when I get out of the game, I'm going to run over him with a car."

Bob Saberhagen, father of Royals pitcher Bret Saberhagen (on Bret's toughness):

>"Anyone who stays in there to watch his baby born has guts. I gave his mother a bullet to bite on and went for a walk when Bret was born."

Ron Hunt, former major league second baseman (about his major league record for being hit by a pitch 243 times in his career):

>"Some people give their bodies to science; I gave mine to baseball."

Billy Martin, manager, Yankees (about fans at Yankee Stadium):

>"If one of them jumps out of the stands like the other night, I'd punch him out in a Minnesota second."

Stan Williams, former major league pitcher (about how he would deal with today's hitters who dig in at the plate):

"I'd walk off the mound, tell him it was a nice hole he was digging, but suggest he make it at least six feet deep because he was going to be buried in it."

Dennis Martinez, pitcher, Baltimore Orioles (about Manager Earl Weaver):
"If he has to bite you to win a game, he'll do it."

Dickie Noles, pitcher, Chicago Cubs (about his drinking habits during his early years in the major leagues):
"I could put away three cases of beer a night. Now I can't handle that much. If I have only 15 beers, I'm totally gone."

Dave Winfield, outfielder, Yankees (about fear):
"Only the laundry man will know how scared I was."

Bill Lee, former major league pitcher (about Boston Red Sox teammates Rick Burleson and Rico Petrocelli):
"When the Iranians were holding our embassy people captive, instead of the Marines we should have sent Burleson and Petrocelli over there. They would have come back in 48 hours with the hostages, the ayatollah and a couple of million barrels of oil."

Macho Mets, 1986

Davey Johnson, manager:
"We're probably the cockiest team in the league. I think other teams feel that, and they come after us. But we enjoy fighting. If that's what it takes, we'll fight every team. You can't push us around."

"You ain't seen nothing yet. We just use our fists on the field. We practice with knives when we're in the clubhouse."

Randy Niemann, relief pitcher (after the Mets jumped to a 7-0 lead after four innings):
"I was bored to death. I started spitting on myself just to have fun."

Bruce Berenyi, pitcher:
"I decided to grow a beard to scare the batters a bit."

Tom Niedenfuer, pitcher, Dodgers (about being roughed up in a fight with the Mets' Ray Knight):
"There's a lot of long fingernails in this league."

Post-Baseball Macho

While many baseball players stay in the game after retiring by moving into some form of management, many others do not. There are other worlds to conquer for those macho enough to try.

Bernie Carbo represents one direction players can take. Carbo, who is best remembered for his pinch-hit, three-run homer that helped the Red Sox beat the Reds in Game 6 of the 1975 World Series, was released by the Cardinals in 1980. At that point, Bernie decided to start a new career—as a hairdresser. After one month at cosmetology school, Carbo said: "I think it's going to be all right. I did my first set today."

Randy Poffo decided to go in a different direction when his playing career came to an end. After being signed to a minor league contract in the Cardinals' organization in 1971, Poffo spent three years in the lower reaches of the Cards' farm system. The switch-hitting catcher-outfielder, who earned the moniker "Macho Man" for his tough style of play, then spent brief periods with Cincinnati and Chicago White Sox affiliates before getting his final release in 1975. It was time to consider another line of work.

Below is a picture of young Randy with the Orangeburg Cardinals. To find out what happened to Randy Poffo after his baseball career ended, you'll have to turn the page.

Professional wrestler Randy (Macho Man) Savage and Elizabeth.

Kiner's Korner

"That's the great thing about baseball: You never know what's going on."—Ralph Kiner.

Ralph Kiner was one of the greatest home run hitters in baseball history. In only 10 seasons in the major leagues, Ralph hit 369 home runs and drove in 1,015 runs. As a member of the Pittsburgh Pirates, Kiner won or shared the National League home run crown his first seven seasons in the big leagues. In 1947, Kiner hit 51 homers and drove in 127 runs while batting .313. Two years later, Kiner hit 54 homers and again drove in 127 runs while batting .310. In 34 games in his career, Ralph hit two or more home runs. He hit three homers in a game three times, and twice he blasted five homers in two consecutive games. Kiner also totaled 13 grand slams, and he is the only player ever to hit homers in three consecutive All-Star Games. He was inducted into baseball's Hall of Fame in 1975.

Those credentials are plenty for one man, but as a capper to a long and meritorious playing career, Ralph Kiner became a New York Mets announcer and the host of the Mets' postgame television show, "Kiner's Korner." It is in this capacity that Kiner has gained even greater fame.

In the very first year of the Mets' existence (1962), in the very first "Kiner's Korner" show, Ralph interviewed Mets Manager Casey Stengel. Casey was great, as always, and so was Ralph. But when Casey got up to leave after the interview, he forgot to take off his microphone. Suddenly, the very first set for "Kiner's Korner" came tumbling down around them. And the laughs haven't stopped—or even slowed down—for a quarter of a century.

Kiner Klassics

(About a pair of Montreal Expos pitchers):
"The righthander is Charlie Lea and the lefthander is Bill Lee. One of them comes from another country, and the other one comes from another world."

(About Cincinnati's Riverfront Stadium, which opened in 1970):
"Baseball began right here in this very stadium back in 1869."

(About Mets pitchers Jesse Orosco and Doug Sisk):
". . . a history of sore armness."

(About Orosco not getting a save):
"He did not pitch three innings. And he came in without the on-deck batter being a batter that he would face in his next approach to pitching to the hitter."

(About Chicago's Wrigley Field):
". . . very tough to hit a homer at Wrigley Field because of the wind. You've got to drive it under the wind."

(Generally speaking):
"Tony Gwynn was named Player of the Year for April."

"Nolan Ryan's fastball has been clocked at over 200 miles per hour."

"(Steve) Yeager's uncle is Chuck Yeager, the first man to crash through the sound barrier."

"OK, we need a sound check. Mike (Torrez), count to 10. OK, Mookie (Wilson), you can count to . . . uh, uh. Say your name."

"There's Jim Fanning, the new Montreal manager who replaced Jeff Reardon (Expos relief pitcher)."

"That was Johnnie LeMaster's first hit of the year against the Mets after 19 at-bats in which he went 0-for-19."

"The (Hall of Fame) ceremonies are on the 31st and 32nd (of July)."

"Cesar Cedeno pleaded innocent to charges of running into a car."

"The Pirates won eight of their 102 losses against the Mets last year."

"If Casey Stengel were alive today, he'd be spinning in his grave."

Kiner Kalls

With the thousands of names Kiner has had to pronounce in his ca-

reer, it's no wonder there have been a few fluffs along the way. For instance, Ralph once called:

George Foster—"George Fisher"
George Foster—"George Strawberry"
Darryl Strawberry—"Darryl Throneberry"
Dwight Gooden—"Greg Goossen"
Dwight Gooden—"Dwight Goodman"
Roy Lee Jackson—"Roy Lee Jefferson"
Howard Johnson—"Walter Johnson"
Ray Knight—"Ray Nat"
Dave Kingman—"Ed Kranepool"
Vince Coleman—"Gary Coleman"
Steve (Bedrock) Bedrosian—"Hardrock Bedrosian"
Gary Carter—"Gary Cooper"
Jack Clark—"Jack Carter"
Brent Gaff—"Frank Brent"
Milt May—"Mel Ott"
Joe Price—"Joe Page"
Tim McCarver—"Tim MacArthur"
Bill Madlock—"Bill Maddox"
Larry McWilliams—"Larry McDaniels"
Dan Driessen—"Diane Driessen"
Tucker Ashford—"Tucker Ashburn"
Dann Bilardello—"Don Bordello"

More Krazy Kalls

Charlton Heston—"Charles Heston"
Sir Lawrence Olivier—"Sir Lawrence Oliver"
Marie Osmond—"Marie Osburg"
Golden Gate Bridge—"Golden State Bridge"
National anthem—"New York Anthem"
Mother's Day—"Father's Day"
Ralph Kiner—"Ralph Korner"

Kiner Konfusion

In konklusion, konsider these kernels from assorted Kiner play-by-play broadkasts:

"Andre Dawson (of the Expos) with a two-run home run. And the Phillies lead, 2-0."

"There's a base hit into center field as Santana can't get to it. But he gets over there and makes the catch."

"And the first pitch to (Kevin) Mitchell, lined into right field, deep right field. It's out of here! Off the wall."

"Leading off for the Mets will be Walter Johnson. Make that Howard Johnson. Well, Walter was a good hitter, too."

"There's a curveball. He (Tug McGraw) seldom throws the curve. He probably throws it more now than he ever has."

"He hits it way back. It could be gone. It is gone. Goodbye. Darryl Strawberry with a lop-opposite field home run."

"It's looped into left-center field. Here comes Heep. He can't get to it. He did get to it. Danny Heep with a shoestring catch."

"The ball hit into right field. Strawberry there. He's got a play at first base. (Juan) Samuel didn't know where it was. He was decoyed by Samuel. And they get him at first. What a job by Samuel falling for the trick and being doubled off at first."

"It's going, it's going, it's going . . . to be caught."

Dressed for Success

"It's 100 degrees. And plus, you've got a lot of beaches in San Diego. Some of them are nude beaches. Why would someone want to watch someone in uniform when they could watch somebody nude?"—Pete Rose, manager, Cincinnati Reds.

A Diamond of Many Colors

Baseball's most flamboyant uniforms came about in the '80s. Not the 1980s, mind you, but the 1880s—1882 to be exact. It was that year that the National League adopted the color-by-position regulation.

The only way a particular team could be identified was by the coloring of the stockings. All teams wore white pants, white belts and white ties, but the colors of their caps and shirts were determined by the defensive positions. For example, all pitchers, regardless of team, wore the same colored shirts and caps. Specifically, the 1882 National League color scheme for caps and shirts was:

>   P—Light blue
>   C—Scarlet
>   1B—Scarlet and white
>   2B—Orange and black
>   SS—Maroon
>   3B—Gray and white
>   LF—White
>   CF—Red and black
>   RF—Gray

Confusion reigned, however, and the color-by-position uniforms lasted only one season.

Maybe Numbers Would Be Better

Rather than use colors to identify players, an idea developed to match each player on a team with his own number. Many players objected to the wearing of numbers, however, saying that it made them feel like convicts. As a new century dawned, baseball uniforms still did not have numbers stitched on them.

Numbers finally became worn on a regular basis in 1929, and the team that made it fashionable was the New York Yankees. The reigning world champions wore large numbers on the backs of their uniforms both at home and on the road. The numbers, incidentally, corresponded to each player's position in the batting order. So, when the Yankees' No. 3 batter, Babe Ruth, and cleanup batter Lou Gehrig donned numbered uniforms for the first time in 1929, they wore Nos. 3 and 4, respectively—numbers that have since become legendary.

Fashion Show and Tell

Yogi Berra, coach, Houston Astros:
"Uniforms don't matter. What the hell? You got to wear them. That's the rules."

Fred Claire, executive vice president, Los Angeles Dodgers:
"The most amazing thing I've ever seen was Jay Johnstone, in uniform, in line at a concession stand in Dodger Stadium after a game had already started."

Robin Roberts, pitcher, Yankees (about having his former number retired by the Philadelphia Phillies during spring training in 1962):
"It was very touching. The Yankees were playing the Phillies in spring training, and the Phillies had a ceremony at the Causeway Motel in Tampa. And everybody cried—especially the National League hitters."

Tony Kubek, broadcaster and former Yankee shortstop (about Yankees Owner George Steinbrenner's decision to retire Billy Martin's number):
"I think George wants to retire all numbers. He wants to have his players wear letters, a first for baseball. He could have a diphthong on first base, a vowel on second and, who knows, maybe an umlaut on third. He could have an A team, a B team, a DH on his designated hitter each day and a BP on his bullpen pitcher. He might retire Don Mattingly's number next year."

Mike Lupica, New York Daily News:
"Steinbrenner must stand there in his jammies in the morning and think, 'Should I stick pop tarts in the toaster oven first or retire another number?' "

Ron Kittle, outfielder, Chicago White Sox (about finding out that he had just been traded to the Yankees):
"I'll do the best I can with the Yankees. At least they have better-looking uniforms. The White Sox uniforms are great if you like softball."

Steve Daly, Chicago Tribune (about the White Sox's new uniforms and star player Greg Luzinski):
  "The old uniform made the Sox look like an industrial softball team in Moline. . . . But now the Bull looks like a box of cereal."

Steve Garvey, first baseman, San Diego Padres (talking about the Padres' new pinstriped uniforms):
  "No longer will I feel like I'm wearing a taco."

Kurt Bevacqua, infielder, Padres (about Garvey):
  "He never gets his uniform dirty. Steve always slides on that stripe that runs down his pants."

Paul Owens, manager, Phillies (about leaving his front-office position to become the team's manager):
  "When I went back onto the field and put on the uniform again, I felt out of place—like a guy on a beach in a tuxedo."

Rollie Fingers, pitcher, Milwaukee Brewers (about playing the Yankees in the 1981 American League East playoffs):
  "They've got pinstripes and we've got pinstripes, and in a short series, anything can happen."

Chuck Pool, assistant director of public relations, Astros (about the team's rainbow uniforms):
  "Dan Jenkins wrote that he wondered if the Astros still wore the flag of a Third World country."

Ron Guidry, pitcher, Yankees (to new teammate Wayne Tolleson on his first day with New York):
  "Number 2. Nobody's worn that number around here in awhile."
  (Dale Berra wore Number 2 until being waived by the Yankees only four days earlier.)

Doug Rader, manager, Texas Rangers (about pitcher Tom Henke):
  "He has settled down. He's got confidence. He's throwing strikes, changing speeds and looks good in his uniform."

Gary Nicholson, trainer, Seattle Mariners:
  "Maybe we've come of age. Somebody wants our uniforms."

Harry Caray, announcer, Chicago Cubs (about ballgirl Marla Collins' photo spread in Playboy):
  "That's the best thing I've seen out of uniform this year."

How About in Uniform?

In 1984, outfielder Mel Hall was traded from the Cubs to the Cleveland Indians. When in uniform for his new Indians team, Hall carried six batting gloves, three in each back pocket. When he hit a home run, the fingers of each glove would wave at the opposition as he ran by. Hall also continued to wear his Cubs jacket in Cleveland until A.L. officials made him stop.

Relief pitcher Jim Kern provided some amusing moments with his uniform over the years. He once got carried away when the fans in the stands asked for a baseball. After Kern threw them a ball, they asked for more. So, Kern obliged by throwing them his glove, cap, uniform shirt, sweatshirt, pants, shoes and socks. On other occasions, Kern could be found warming up in the bullpen with his uniform on backward.

Seattle's Gaylord Perry showed considerable foresight before winning his 300th game in 1982. The ancient Mariner changed his uniform during the game so that he would have two uniforms to sell to collectors instead of only one.

Pitcher Sid Fernandez feels right at home when he slips on his New York Mets uniform. Fernandez requested number 50 when he came to New York, and his reasoning was twofold: Fernandez is a native of Hawaii, the 50th state, and his favorite television show is "Hawaii Five-O."

Bill Voiselle.

Carlos May.   *Andy Messersmith.*

Name, Rank and Uniform Number

Pitcher Andy Messersmith signed as a free agent with the Atlanta Braves in 1976. Braves Owner Ted Turner nicknamed Messersmith "Channel" and gave him number 17. Therefore, Messersmith started his Braves career with "Channel 17" on the back of his uniform. It just so happened that Channel 17 also was the TV superstation owned by Turner. N.L. officials eventually saw to it that "Channel" was removed from Messersmith's uniform.

Carlos May of the White Sox wore his birth date on the back of his uniform. Carlos was born May 17, 1948, and he wore number 17. So, the back of the outfielder's uniform read "May 17."

For a few years, Bill Voiselle wore his hometown on the back of his uniform. Voiselle lived in Ninety Six, S.C., and wore number 96.

The Voices
Of Summer

"Branca throws. There's a long fly . . . it's gonna be, I believe . . . the Giants win the pennant! The Giants win the pennant! The Giants win the pennant! The Giants win the pennant! Bobby Thomson hits into the lower deck of the left-field bleachers! The Giants win the pennant, and they're going crazy! They're going crazy! Oooooh! Ooh!"

On October 3, 1951, Bobby Thomson hit The Shot Heard 'Round the World. The New York Giants beat the Brooklyn Dodgers in the third and final playoff game to win the National League pennant. And announcer Russ Hodges uttered possibly the most famous words ever heard in sports.

Over the years, countless major league baseball announcers, both on radio and television, have uttered zillions of words, and a few of them became famous, too. Occasionally, even an infamous word or two somehow managed to sneak in. Two of the most famous practitioners of the latter are announcers Jerry Coleman of the San Diego Padres and Phil (Scooter) Rizzuto of the New York Yankees.

Coleman and Rizzuto have more in common than just the same middle name (Francis) and a knack for using the wrong word. Jerry and Scooter were teammates on the Yankees from 1949-56. Maybe there was something in the water back then. Anyway, Rizzuto played shortstop, Coleman second base, to give the Yanks a solid middle infield. In order for a double-play tandem to click, the players must be able to communicate with each other. And from whom did both of these famous communicators learn the art of communication? Well, it just might have been from their loquacious manager—Casey Stengel. Bearing all this in mind, it makes

MY ENGLISH PERFESSOR WAS "CASEY"

sense that Coleman and Rizzuto almost sound alike—especially when it comes to verbal faux pas. And both announcers have provided more than their share.

First, let's head out to San Diego and tune in to a few choice offerings from the voice of the Padres, Jerry Coleman:
"There's a fly ball deep to center field. Winfield is going back, back. He hits his head against the wall. It's rolling back toward second base. This is a terrible thing for the Padres."

"Grubb goes back, back. He's under the warning track."

"George Hendrick simply lost that sun-blown pop-up."

"Young Frank Pastore may have just pitched the biggest victory of 1979, maybe the biggest victory of the year."

"On the mound is Randy Jones, the lefthander with the Karl Marx hairdo."

"Rich Folkers is throwing up in the bullpen."

"Those amateur umpires are sure flexing their fangs tonight."

"Enos Cabell started out here with the Astros. And before that he was with the Orioles."

"Benedict may not be hurt as much as he really is."

"We're all sad to see Glenn Beckert leave. Before he goes, though, I hope he stops by so we can kiss him goodbye. He's that kind of guy."

"If Rose's streak was still intact, with that single to left, the fans would be throwing babies out of the upper deck."

"He slides into second with a stand-up double."

Now let's move across the country to New York, where Phil Rizzuto has been treating Yankee fans to colorful commentary since 1957:
"Italians are very romantic, a very arduous people."

"I think there should be a rule that in September there should be no extra-inning games allowed."

"If Don Mattingly isn't the American League MVP, nothing's kosher in China."

"You gotta be partial up here (in the booth); or is it impartial?"

"Two balls, two strikes, two runs in for the Yankees. (Crack of bat.) Jammed him. That went pretty far for a jam job. Oh! It went . . . holy cow! I don't . . . it jammed him. A home run. I . . . the old eyes are gone! Holy cow! I'm going home. I've got to get my eyes examined."

"I can't see. And I can't hear. And I don't know what's going on."

More Scooterisms

After playing in the major leagues for 13 years and then more than doubling that in the broadcast booth, Phil Rizzuto often is asked if he would consider becoming a manager. The Scooter lets everyone know that he wants no part of that scene. "There are three things that dictate against it," he said. "I don't chew tobacco, I don't like sunflower seeds and the dugout steps are too high for me."

The Scooter is by no means the only announcer in the Yankees' radio and TV booth. Columnist Phil Mushnick came up with a baseball description of the Yankees' radio team: "The Yanks, heard over WABC, use five guys. It's the only radio booth with an on-deck circle."

As Rizzuto has pointed out, sometimes it's even dangerous up in the booth: "We've got so many announcers that I got spiked the other day."

Here are a few conversations that the Scooter has had with some of those many Yankee announcers:

Rizzuto: "Reggie's home run has gone clear out of the ball park."

Bill White: "Actually, Scooter, that ball landed in the seats."

Rizzuto: "It doesn't matter. They can't see it anyway at home."

Fran Healy: "We're journalists. We're pros."

Rizzuto: "Yes, but you gotta make up things once in awhile."

Rizzuto: "There's a foul ball smashed into the Yankee dugout. Boy, I hope that's not Guidry who got in the way."

Frank Messer: "Scooter, uh, Guidry is on the mound."

Rizzuto: "You know, Frank, you're right."

Healy: "When I was playing, we all used to be like Pavlov's dogs whenever we faced expansion teams."

Rizzuto: "What on earth does that mean?"

Healy: "All of us used to salivate on our way up to home plate."

Rizzuto: "What are you wiping off (my face), Mick? A bread crumb?"

Mickey Mantle: "I think it was a booger."

White: "I think Johnny Neun used to be a Yankee manager."

Rizzuto: "You must be kidding. I didn't know that." (Johnny Neun managed the Yankees for 14 games in 1946—when Phil Rizzuto was the Yankees' shortstop.)

Bon Mots From the Booth

"I know what this gutless business is all about. It is a life style of back stabbing. I just don't need it. If it weren't for the dollars, I wouldn't be in network TV."—Don Drysdale, Hall of Fame pitcher.

Don Drysdale, ABC-TV announcer:

"They've had some standing-room seats on sale."

Lou Brock, Chicago White Sox announcer:

"I'm learning to do something that for me is turning out to be one of the toughest things I've ever tried—keeping score."

Fred White, Kansas City Royals announcer (upon seeing a typographical error indicating that Minnesota Twins pitcher Terry Felton started the game and also came in to pitch in relief):

"Well, I see in the game in Minnesota that Terry Felton has relieved himself on the mound in the second inning."

Harry Kalas, Philadelphia Phillies announcer (about Phillies center fielder Garry Maddox):
"He's turned his life around. He used to be depressed and miserable. Now he's miserable and depressed."

Al Michaels, ABC-TV announcer:
"I'm waiting for the day we see the 'wave' at the Metropolitan Opera."

Bill White, Yankees announcer:
"Winfield robbed Armas of at least a home run."

Byrum Saam, Phillies announcer:
"Most people up here (Montreal) speak French. However, they are nice people."

Spencer Ross, Yankees announcer:
"The Oakland Athletics have just won the rubber game of this four-game series."

Vin Scully, Dodgers announcer:
"Alejandro's stuff is as good as Mario Soto's, but Alejandro is a
little eccentric and marches to a different Walkman."

Jimmy Piersall, White Sox announcer:
"You know why I called (umpire) Ken Kaiser a whale? Because
he is a whale. That's why."

Roy Firestone, ESPN talk-show host:
"I'm sure a lot of you know what (NBC sportscaster) Marv Albert sounds like. He sounds like he swallowed lye."

Lorn Brown, White Sox announcer (with a casual anecdote between
pitches):
"White Sox fans may remember Alan Bannister, who was with
the White Sox. When he was with Arizona State, he went with
the college All-Star team to Japan, and the Japanese do not slide
going into second, and he wound up hitting a Japanese baserun-
ner between the eyes (actually the side of the head), and in fact
killed him. Here's the 2-1 pitch, and it's low, a ball. . . ."

Billy Martin, Yankees announcer (responding to Royals Manager
Dick Howser, who said Billy had it made with his new announcing job
that required only 90-second pregame and postgame shows):
"The thing is, Dick doesn't know how tough it can be when you
don't know how to read."

Steve Zabriskie, New York Mets announcer (describing a pop-up):
"It's playable—if it stays in play."

Red Barber, Brooklyn Dodgers announcer (when Yankees pitcher Bill
Bevens' 1947 World Series no-hitter was broken up in the bottom of
the ninth inning by pinch-hitter Cookie Lavagetto's two-out, game-
winning double):
"I'll be a suck-egg mule."

Bob Uecker, Milwaukee Brewers announcer:
"My ultimate desire outside of baseball would be to broadcast
wars—live."

The All-Announcer Team
"If a young guy asked me for advice on how to get into

broadcasting, I'd say, 'Hit .350 or win the Heisman.' "—
Skip Caray, announcer, Atlanta Braves.

None of the broadcasters listed below won college football's Heisman
Trophy, but they all excelled in major league baseball. Submitted for
your approval, the All-Announcer Team:

> C—Johnny Bench, CBS Radio
> 1B—Harmon Killebrew, KMSP-TV (Twins)
> 2B—Joe Morgan, GiantsVision (San Francisco Giants)
> 3B—Brooks Robinson, WMAR-TV (Baltimore Orioles)
> SS—Phil Rizzuto, WABC Radio, WPIX-TV, Sports Channel
>   (Yankees)
> OF—Duke Snider, CFCF Radio, CBMT-TV (Montreal
>   Expos)
> OF—Mickey Mantle, Sports Channel (Yankees)
> OF—Al Kaline, WDIV-TV (Detroit Tigers)
> DH—Ken Singleton, The Sports Network (Expos, Toronto
>   Blue Jays)
> PH—Ralph Kiner, WOR-TV, Sports Channel (Mets)
> RHP—Jim Palmer, ABC-TV
> RHP—Don Drysdale, ABC-TV, WFLD-TV, Sportsvision
>   (White Sox)
> LHP—Herb Score, WWWE Radio (Cleveland Indians)
> LHP—Jim Kaat, WPIX-TV (Yankees)
> REL—Al Hrabosky, Cencom (St. Louis Cardinals)
> MGR—Lou Boudreau, WGN Radio (Chicago Cubs)

Competition was tough. Those who did not make the All-Announcer
Team—which consisted of radio and TV announcers who worked on
broadcasts of major league games in 1986—include a Hall of Famer
(George Kell), a Most Valuable Player (Joe Torre), a Cy Young
Award winner (Steve Stone), a two-time batting champion (Richie
Ashburn), a two-time no-hit pitcher (Steve Busby) and a four-
decade player (Tim McCarver), not to mention Billy Martin and the
fans' favorite, Bob Uecker.

I Smell a Rat

The first sporting event ever televised was a baseball game between
Princeton and Columbia in 1939. Director Harry Coyle was not along
for that one, but he was in the control booth when the World Series
was televised for the first time in 1947, and he has been along to direct
World Series games many times since then.

Coyle's job is to sit in the television truck during the game and quickly but carefully decide which camera angle offers the best picture at any given moment. Every picture the viewer sees at home is selected by the venerable Coyle.

In 1975, the world was treated to an especially memorable World Series. The Cincinnati Reds beat the Boston Red Sox in seven games, but it was Game 6 that was acclaimed by many to be the most exciting sporting event ever televised. Boston's Carlton Fisk hit a home run in the bottom of the 12th inning that tied the Series at three games each. The Reds came back to win Game 7 and the World Series, but the final contest was almost anticlimactic.

Harry Coyle won an Emmy Award for the dramatic shots of Fisk waving and coaxing his long drive to stay fair. The talented Coyle certainly was deserving of his Emmy, but the real reason he got the shot of Fisk was because of a frightened cameraman and a rat. Now, some would contend that rats are not uncommon in the TV business, but when was the last time you saw a frightened cameraman?

Here's the scoop. Lou Gerard was manning the camera that NBC had stationed inside the scoreboard in the left-field wall at Boston's Fenway Park. Gerard's job was to follow any ball that was hit toward the Green Monster, but on Fisk's game-ending drive, Gerard froze in his tracks. Sitting atop his camera—and glaring him in the eye—was a rat.

Stunned by the rodent's sudden appearance literally in front of his eyes, Gerard didn't move. Meanwhile, the camera continued to focus on the antics of Carlton Fisk, ignoring the ball that was soaring down the left-field line. This particular reaction shot, shown to the world by director Harry Coyle, led the way to a revolutionary style of TV coverage of sporting events.

According to Coyle

One more tidbit, directed your way, concerns master director Coyle. The 1984 World Series, televised by NBC, opened in San Diego. But with the Padres playing the Cubs in San Diego in the final three games of the ABC-televised National League Championship Series, Harry Coyle and his crew could not even set up until the last minute.

When Coyle and company finally were allowed to set up for the opening game between the Padres and the Tigers, Harry said he felt like an

Iranian trespasser. When asked to explain, he replied: "You know, caught between Iraq and a hard place."

Talking Hairdos

ESPN:
> "Bert Blyleven won his sixth in a row to up his record to 5-1."

"Good Morning America" (to California Angels rookie Wally Joyner):
> "You can go on right after Darryl Raspberry."

Local TV (to Texas Rangers Manager Doug Rader):
> Reporter: "Doug, how do you think Honeycutt will do for the team this year?"
> Rader: "I don't think he'll do much for us since he'll be playing for the Dodgers."

Local TV (to Red Sox pitcher Roger Clemens):
> Reporter: "What will it be like to pitch against a team (Seattle Mariners) that you struck out 30 against?"
> Clemens: "It was 20."
> Reporter: "Well, 20 last time, maybe 30 this time."

Say Good Night, Dick

Bogdan Chruscicki, Polish radio announcer:
> "Baseball was designed for American television—15 seconds of action and three-minute breaks for commercials."

Jim Bouton, author and former major league pitcher:
> "If TV executives ever got Hemingway's 'Old Man and the Sea,' they'd say: 'Ernie, we love you. But the part about the fishing is boring. And the man is too old. He should have a girlfriend.' "

Dusty Rhodes, former Giants outfielder (comparing a home run to Howard Cosell's short-lived variety show):
> "That home run stayed in the air longer than Howard's variety show stayed on the air."

Johnny Carson, host, "The Tonight Show":
> "If the World Series goes seven games, it will be NBC's longest-running show this fall."

Dave Bristol, coach, Phillies (discussing Pete Rose's chances to catch

Ty Cobb two years before the record was broken):
> "ESPN might be the one thing that keeps Pete Rose from breaking Ty Cobb's hit record. He stays up all night every night watching it."

Tim Flannery, infielder, Padres (about San Diego winning the 1984 N.L. pennant):
> "What we've done has never been done in San Diego. And I know we've done it because I've got it on videotape. Unless someone erases it, I mean."

Paul Owens, manager, Phillies (about having to get up early three times in 11 days to appear on "Good Morning America" and "Today" to talk about his N.L. championship team in 1983):
> "I'm sick and tired of getting up early. Doesn't Johnny Carson want to talk to me?"

Buddy Biancalana, shortstop, Royals (about talk-show host David Letterman's constant teasing about Buddy's base-hit total):
> "I'm still a lot closer to Rose than he is in pursuit of Johnny Carson."

Dave LaPoint, pitcher, Tigers:
> "My goal in life is to be on 'Cheers,' sitting next to Normie, talking to Sam Malone."

Lon Simmons, Oakland A's announcer:
> "I don't know if the A's are paid up in their medical insurance or not, but they better hope they are. Alfredo Griffin is taped up like he should be lying inside a pyramid."

Mel Allen, Yankees announcer:
> "Isn't it odd that in the communications field you seem to have the biggest breakdown in communications of any business?"

Baseball
By the Numbers

"Statistics are about as interesting as first-base coaches."
—Jim Bouton, author and former major league pitcher.

Arithmetic 101

Steve Sax, second baseman, Los Angeles Dodgers:
"When I'm hitting good, 80 percent of the time I'm going up the middle, 20 percent of the time to right and 20 percent of the time to left."

Frank Pastore, pitcher, Cincinnati Reds:
"The season's only eight games old, and we're 5-2. I'll take that anytime."

Claude Osteen, coach, Philadelphia Phillies (about the Baltimore Orioles' Mike Boddicker, who pitched against the Phillies in the 1983 World Series):
"The kid has four pitches that he throws four different ways. That gives him 12 pitches."

Rickey Henderson, outfielder, New York Yankees (about his first trip back to Oakland since leaving the A's, plus the presence of Manager Billy Martin, who also used to be with the A's):
"I figure two-thirds of the people will come out to see me, two-thirds will come out to see Billy and two-thirds will come out to see the Yankees."

Dave Beard, pitcher, Maine Guides (International):
"You feel all alone out there. You really do, because you're seeing only one person. You're seeing the catcher and the hitter."

Bill Madden, sportswriter, New York Daily News:
"Righetti bore down and struck out John Wathan on a 3-1 pitch."

Warren Cromartie, outfielder, Montreal Expos (about teammate Al Oliver's two grand slams in nine days):
"That's like getting seven or eight RBIs in two games."

Pat Gillick, general manager, Toronto Blue Jays (about the Detroit

Tigers' incredible 35-5 start in 1984):
"If we were 41-0, we'd have a 2½-game lead on the Tigers."

Hank Aguirre, pitcher, Tigers:
"I got one hit in three years, and I thought I was batting .333."

Joe Cowley, pitcher, Yankees (about the 1985 pennant race):
"We're not out of it yet, and even when we are, hopefully the guy who figures it all up isn't that good in arithmetic."

Statistically Speaking

Toby Harrah, infielder, Texas Rangers:
"Statistics are like a girl in a fine bikini. It shows a lot, but it doesn't show everything."

Vin Scully, announcer, Dodgers:
"Statistics are used by baseball fans in much the same way that a drunk leans against a street lamp; it's there more for support than for enlightenment."

Robin Fuson, pitcher, Maine Guides:
"I was hoping the fans would see that 23.60 (earned-run average) on the scoreboard and figure the decimal was in the wrong place."

Walt Terrell, pitcher, Tigers:
"You can take that ERA stuff and stick it as far as you can stick it. The name of the game is winning as far as I'm concerned. I'm not an ERA fan at all. They don't give out Cy Young Awards to ERA winners."

Ricky Horton, pitcher, St. Louis Cardinals:
"If my ERA is under my batting average (.058 at the time), I'd be happy the rest of my life."

Roger LaFrancois, catcher, Boston Red Sox (about a 1982 season in which he spent the entire year in Boston but had only 10 at-bats):
"I'm probably the only guy in baseball who can describe every hit he had last year. I can tell you the team we were playing, the inning, the pitcher, the count, what I hit and what pitches I had been thrown before the hit."

Rudy May, pitcher, Yankees:
"I know my days are numbered. I just don't know the number."

Damaso Garcia, second baseman, Blue Jays (after a four-game spree in which he went 10-for-18 with nine runs batted in as the team's leadoff batter):
"I'm going to go on a hunger strike in two days if (Manager) Bobby (Cox) doesn't hit me fourth."

Dave Winfield, outfielder, Yankees:
"Now that we're at .500, there's only two ways to go."

John Lowenstein, outfielder, Orioles:
"World War III would render all baseball statistics meaningless."

Tommy John, pitcher, Yankees:
"The only figure I like to talk about is my wife's."

In Pursuit of the Almighty Dollar

"Back home in Puerto Rico, it used to be that mothers would tell their sons to put down their bats and gloves and come in and read their books and homework. After all the money that's floating around, the mothers say, 'Put down those books and get out there with the ball and bat.'" — Jose Morales, pinch-hitter, Los Angeles Dodgers.

In 1986, the average salary of all major league baseball players on the opening-day rosters, including those on the disabled list, was $431,521. Despite the players' cry of collusion among major league owners, this figure represented a generous salary increase from 1985, when the opening-day average salary was only $364,677.

Money Talks

Steve Garvey, first baseman, San Diego Padres:
"When I was playing for Ogden, Utah, Tom Lasorda told me: 'You're going to be a star in this game. You're going to make $50,000 a year!' And I thought, 'Gee, that would be nice.'"

Tom Lasorda, manager, Dodgers:
"Fernando Valenzuela now makes $1 million a year. Three years ago, Valenzuela's alarm clock was a rooster."

"Back then, when he (rookie Valenzuela) got paid, he used to count it. Now when he gets paid, he weighs it."

"He (Ron Cey) was making $400 a month when I first met him. The other day he wrote out a check and it was returned by the bank. It was marked, 'Insufficient funds; not yours, but ours.'"

Reggie Jackson, outfielder, California Angels:
"Most people can't afford to live where I live, and that's why I live there."

Cal Ripken, shortstop, Baltimore Orioles:
"I'm basically practical, but sometimes I think that, just for a week, I'd like to have a cook and a chauffeur and everything, just to see what it would be like. Then I'd go back to being normal."

Dave Winfield, outfielder, New York Yankees:
  "After withholding, one of my checks is about equal to the gross of what my mother in St. Paul could make in about four years at her job."

George Bamberger, manager, Milwaukee Brewers:
  "Now I know you can't put on a salary drive because so many of you have long-term contracts. So why don't you put on a personal-pride drive?"

Tim McCarver, announcer, New York Mets (about the St. Louis Cardinals' Ozzie Smith, a light-hitting shortstop who had signed a contract worth $2 million per year):
  "Two million a year could make you stronger. Or you could buy someone else to hit for you."

Lou Piniella, outfielder, Yankees (to teammate Catfish Hunter):
  "Hey, Catfish, I know how (Owner George) Steinbrenner can get back all the money he paid you. All he has to do is sell insurance to the people sitting in the right-field seats when you pitch."

Pete Rose, player-manager, Cincinnati Reds (when presented with a red Corvette):
  "Now I don't know what to do with the $170,000 worth of Porsches I have at home."

Amos Otis, outfielder, Kansas City Royals (arguing for a higher salary):
  "I put all those people in the park who come to boo me."

Gary Carter, catcher, Montreal Expos:
  "If the Expos come up with an offer I can't refuse, I wouldn't turn it down."

Vendor, Shea Stadium:
  "Get your scorecard—names and numbers of all the millionaires."

Contract Incentives: The Santa Clause

"We feel a player getting one, two, three or $400,000 a year doesn't need incentive to play. I need incentive to pay him."—Buzzie Bavasi, general manager, Angels.

Dwayne Murphy of the Oakland A's once signed a contract in which he would receive $2,000 each month that he weighed less than 200 pounds. The outfielder had never weighed 200 pounds in his entire life.

Don Robinson of the Pittsburgh Pirates negotiated a contract that would pay him an extra $100,000 if he never weighed more than 225 pounds. The more Don thought about the deal he had made (and the more he thought about dessert), the less he liked it. The pitcher went back to the Pirates and renegotiated his weight clause. The weight limit was upped from 225 to 235 pounds.

In 1983, Pittsburgh third baseman Bill Madlock also had a weight stipulation, and don't think teammate Steve Nicosia didn't know about it. Said the Pirate catcher: "My whole salary is less than what Bill Madlock can make from his weight clause."

Richard Dotson of the Chicago White Sox was offered a bonus of $25,000 if he won the Silver Slugger award, which is presented at the end of the season to each league's best hitter at each position. There's only one catch: Richard Dotson is a pitcher in the American League, which uses the designated hitter.

Ernie Whitt, catcher, Toronto Blue Jays:
"Incentive clauses give you, well, incentive."

Jack McKeon, general manager, Padres (about incentive bonuses):
"We feel that you pay a guy for a 162-game schedule, so why pay him extra for playing 150 games?"

"You're paying a guy a fantastic salary. What is it for, showing up at the ball park?"

Arbitration: Here Come Da Judge

When players and management fail to agree to terms of a new contract, arbitration is used to break the impasse. In arbitration, the player submits the salary figure he thinks he deserves while team officials submit the figure they believe the player should be paid. A neutral third party—the arbitrator—then approves one of the figures, and both the player and the team officials must abide by the arbitrator's decision.

To a great extent, arbitration is responsible (along with free agency) for the skyrocketing salaries in baseball. Several players have been awarded huge raises after posting a strong season or two. But players don't always win. For instance, outfielder Pedro Guerrero was understandably upset when an arbitrator approved the Dodgers' contract offer in a 1983 arbitration hearing. But Guerrero's reaction seemed a bit harsh: "I hope the jerk who made that decision, the arbitrator, dies."

Mets pitcher Ron Darling also lost at arbitration, despite the fact that he was coming off an excellent 1985 season. At least one fan was sympathetic to Darling's plight. New Jersey lawyer Robert Mellman had seen the arbitrator in Darling's case, Roger Abrams, show similar judgment many years before—when Abrams was his law professor at Case Western Reserve University. Said Mellman: "I wrote a final exam paper, worthy of an A-plus. Abrams gave me a C. Professor Abrams has a habit of underestimating great talent."

The case of Mike Edwards vs. the A's had an interesting twist. Edwards was Oakland's starting second baseman in 1978 and '79, and having worked for the penurious Charlie Finley, he decided his only chance to make more money was to go to arbitration. So, Edwards asked for $50,000. When asked to submit a counteroffer, Finley offered $56,000. Because the team had offered more than the player had requested, the arbitration was withdrawn.

Secret Agent Man

Dave Winfield, Yankees:
> "These days baseball is different. You come to spring training, you get your legs ready, your arm loose, your agent ready, your lawyer lined up."

Frank Robinson, manager, San Francisco Giants (about a club rule

that made the clubhouse off limits one hour before the game instead
of only 30 minutes):
> "They (players) need time to catch up on the stock market and
> check with their agents."

Ed Gottlieb, agent (after negotiating Ozzie Smith's $2 million con-
tract):
> "Ozzie wants me to go to the Soviet Union and negotiate disar-
> mament."

Executive Decisions

Ken Landreaux, outfielder, Dodgers:
> "Winning isn't as important as doing well individually. You can't
> take teamwork up to the front office to negotiate."

Anonymous general manager (about the signing of free agents):
> "Negotiations are going to be like nuclear warfare. In the end,
> nobody wins."

Bill Veeck (after selling the White Sox):
> "I don't mind the high price of stardom. I just don't like the high
> price of mediocrity."

Of Princes and Paupers

Pitcher Vida Blue has made millions of dollars playing baseball. But
he was looking to save a little more cash if the Giants decided to play
some of their games in Oakland in 1986. "I'm all for it," he said. "I'll
save 75 cents in bridge tolls."

Outfielder Jim Hickman, a 13-year veteran of the major leagues, once
admitted that he would have been almost as happy working in the
cotton mills back home in Henning, Tenn., if not for one thing that
made him choose baseball. It wasn't the money. "The lint keeps getting in my nostrils," he said.

Old-Timers' Views

Don Zimmer, coach, Cubs:
> "When I signed my first contract, I got $140 a month. When we
> left on our last road trip, I got meal money for 13 days—$540.
> You think this game hasn't gone crazy?"

Mickey Mantle, Hall of Fame outfielder:

"There are guys making $400,000 a year now who don't even belong in the majors. Do you know that Joe DiMaggio made a total of $700,000 during his career?"

Ted Williams, Hall of Fame outfielder and the last major leaguer to hit .400 for an entire season in 1941:
  "If I was being paid $30,000 a year, the very least I could do was hit .400."

Don Drysdale, Hall of Fame pitcher:
  "When we played, World Series checks meant something. Now all they do is screw up your taxes."

Jimmy Piersall, former major league outfielder:
  "Most of the players today own the hotel. They don't have any roommates."

Monte Irvin, Hall of Fame outfielder:
  "Looking at the contrast in salaries between today and my day, I wish my mamma had better timing."

Lefty Gomez, Hall of Fame pitcher (when the newspapers in New York called him a holdout because he had asked the Yankees for more money):
  "That isn't true. The Yankees are the holdouts. I asked first."

Sparky Anderson, manager, Detroit Tigers:
  "Just one time, I'd like to see a free agent say he signed with a club because they gave him two Brink's trucks. They always say at those news conferences that it's wonderful to be where they are wanted. They don't care where they're wanted; they care where the money is."

Meteorological Illogic

"You can have money piled to the ceiling, but the size of your funeral is going to depend on the weather."—Chuck Tanner, manager, Pittsburgh Pirates.

Despite domed stadiums, Zambonis, artificial turf and automatic tarpaulins, baseball still hasn't figured out how to control the weather. But everyone still has an opinion on it.

On Rain

Peter Ueberroth, commissioner:
> "In the month of April, there was not a single rainout. I made a deal."

Wally Backman, second baseman, New York Mets (about the Mets' 26-7 loss—a game in which New York trailed, 16-0, after only two innings—to the Philadelphia Phillies in 1985):
> "After the second inning, all I could think of was, 'Where's the rain?'"

Tim McCarver, announcer (about the rain during a Mets broadcast):
> "The drops are big, but they're spread wide apart."

And Snow

Tom Lasorda, manager, Los Angeles Dodgers (about his minor league pitching in Montreal):
> "I won 125 games (including playoff victories) and was leading in the fifth inning of five others that were snowed out."

Dave Bergman, first baseman, Detroit Tigers:
> "Snow is difficult during batting practice. You don't know which of the little white things to swing at."

Doug Ault, first baseman, Toronto Blue Jays (about the first game in the history of the franchise, before which there were snow flurries and during which he hit two home runs):
> "If it had snowed all year, I might have hit 60 or 65."

When It's Cold

Doug Sisk, pitcher, Mets:
> "It was cold, a tough day to throw. The ball felt like a pool cue."

Earl Weaver, manager, Baltimore Orioles (about his team having to play while a nearby racetrack was closed because of cold weather):
> "They're not sending the horses out today. Why should I send my thoroughbreds out there today?"

Cal Ripken Sr., manager, Orioles:
> "Sources told me it would be a cold day in Aberdeen (his home in Maryland) when I got this job. And when I got up this morning, it was damn cold."

And When It's Hot

Doug Flynn, infielder, Mets:
> "It was so hot today, the fire hydrants were chasing the dogs."

Jimmy Williams, coach, Orioles (about the drop in temperature at Texas' Arlington Stadium from 106 to 104 degrees):
> "I just went in and put on my jacket."

Pat Corrales, manager, Cleveland Indians (about his habit of wearing a jacket regardless of the temperature):
> "It keeps you cooler. People don't believe me, but have you ever seen a naked Arab?"

And When the Wind Blows and the Fog Swirls

Joe Garagiola, announcer, NBC-TV:
> "The wind always seems to blow against catchers when they are running."

Jerry Dybzinski, Chicago White Sox (about teammate LaMarr Hoyt's 1984 one-hitter against the New York Yankees and Don Mattingly's bloop single in the seventh inning):
> "You could tell from the beginning of the game there was a no-hitter in the wind. However, the wind blew it away."

Gary Pettis, outfielder, California Angels:
> "When the wind is blowing out, you do a lot of praying and somehow hope the wind doesn't blow you into oblivion."

Bobby Cox, manager, Blue Jays (after a wind-blown triple with the bases loaded by Royals catcher Jim Sundberg helped Kansas City beat Toronto in Game 7 of the 1985 American League Championship Series):

"It wasn't experience that beat us. It was the wind. That and the fact that our bats went south on us and we are north."

Dennis (Oil Can) Boyd, pitcher, Boston Red Sox (after a Red Sox-Indians game in Cleveland was stopped because of fog):
"When you build a stadium on the ocean, what can you expect but that you're going to get a game fogged in?"

Mike Brown, pitcher, Red Sox (about the fog):
"Hurt my location, because I wasn't sure just where the location was."

Life in the Bushes

"In Kansas City, I had a phone in my bathroom. In the minors, I stayed in hotels where the fire escape was a rope."—Tony Torchia, coach, Boston Red Sox.

Bush-League Banter

Mickey Mahler, pitcher, Texas Rangers:
    "Every player who has played three straight years in the majors I'd send back to Triple A for a month, just to let them see what it was like so they won't forget how good they have it." (Ironically, the Rangers sent the much-traveled Mahler to their Triple-A team in Oklahoma City the next day.)

Mickey Mahler, Oklahoma City 89ers:
    "Teams think it's chic to release Mickey Mahler."

Wally Backman, second baseman, Tidewater Tides (about starting the 1981 season with the New York Mets and then being sent to the club's International League team):
    "I'd rather be an unpaid major leaguer than a $3,000 a month minor leaguer."

Jim Frey, coach, Mets (recalling a minor league player who was about to be released by longtime player-manager Barney Lutz):
    "The guy pulled out a knife on Barney and says, 'If you're cutting me, I'm cutting you.'"

Jim (Bobo) Breazeale, first baseman, Richmond Braves:
    "He's amphibious. He throws righthanded and lefthanded."

Joe Frazier, manager, Tidewater Tides (when told that Tides pitcher Jerry Cram had compiled an 8-1 record and a 2.88 earned-run average in 1975):
    "If I knew he was that good, I'd have pitched him more."

Joe Lis, first baseman, Toledo Mud Hens (when told that he had won another minor league award):
    "Even my dogs eat out of silver bowls."

Champ Summers, outfielder, Detroit Tigers (when reminded of his minor league days and the muggy weather at Indianapolis):
    "I spent $3,500 on deodorant playing in the league one season."

Rocky Bridges, manager, Prince William Pirates (explaining why he

had finished second in a milking contest before the game):
  "I didn't try too hard. I was afraid I'd get emotionally involved with the cow."

Phil Durkee, International League umpire (to Richmond Braves Manager Scraps Courtney, who was lecturing his pitcher, catcher and entire infield on the mound):
  "Come on, Scraps, you're supposed to take the team picture before the game."

Clint (Scraps) Courtney, manager, Richmond Braves (to pitcher Jimmy Freeman, who was known for his control problems):
  "OK, Freeman, it's your turn next. Go down to the bullpen and get wild."

Jim Marshall, manager, Buffalo Bisons (about pitcher Grady Hall):
  "He has good command of his concentration."

John Kruk, outfielder, San Diego Padres (about playing his first year in the minor leagues at Walla Walla, Wash., after growing up in the small town of Keyser, W.Va.):
  "It was the first time I'd ever had to talk to people I didn't know."

Dennis (Oil Can) Boyd, pitcher, Pawtucket Red Sox (about a brush-back pitch he had thrown after surrendering back-to-back home runs):
  "I just wanted them to know that batting practice ends at 6:30."

Rick Hatcher, pitcher, Durham Bulls (after pitching a perfect game against Salem):
  "It's going to be hard to go out there the next time and do as well."

George Steinbrenner, owner, New York Yankees (about future Cy Young Award winner Ron Guidry, who was pitching at Syracuse in 1976):
  "He's strictly a Triple-A pitcher."

Graig Nettles, third baseman, Yankees (about teammate Dave LaRoche, who once again had been called up from Triple-A Columbus):

"LaRoche is like The Sporting News. He comes out once a week."

Bobby Brown, outfielder, Yankees (when told he was being sent to the minor leagues):
"I'll go to Columbus over my dead body."

John Robertson, columnist, Toronto Sun (about the Yankees' refusal to go to the minor leagues for players until Don Mattingly and a few others finally helped to change their thinking):
"It took Columbus six months to discover America, but it took George Steinbrenner 11 years to discover Columbus."

Brian Sheekey, pitcher, Anderson Tigers (in response to someone who had mentioned that he had charisma):
"Charisma? Maybe I ought to see a doctor."

Earl Weaver, manager, Baltimore Orioles (about optioning Drungo Hazewood to the minors after the outfielder batted .583 in spring training in 1980):
"I've never cut a guy hitting that high before. But he was making the rest of us look bad with that average."

Stuart Revo, chairman of the board, Pittsfield Cubs:
> "I knew an operator who said the ideal minor league season was to win the pennant, go to the playoffs and lose in the last game so you wouldn't have to spend any money for championship rings."

Art Clarkson, general manager, Birmingham Barons (about advertising his club above urinals in restaurants):
> "It's a captive audience."

Winters in Buffalo

You wouldn't think that anyone would ever look forward to or promote "Winters in Buffalo." Well, you're wrong. That's exactly what the Buffalo Bisons of the American Association did.

Matt Winters, a native of Buffalo, signed with the Yankees in 1978 and played in their minor league organization for eight seasons. Then, on November 12, 1985, Winters was released. The Chicago White Sox signed Winters six weeks later and put him on the roster of their Triple-A farm club in Buffalo. Everyone was happy, and the Bisons heavily promoted their newest acquisition for the 1986 American Association season.

Surprise! The White Sox then made a trade with the Yankees in February, and Winters was part of the deal. Matt was taken off the Buffalo roster and added to the Yankees' Triple-A roster in Columbus—where he had played the previous three seasons.

Another surprise followed. The Yankees loaned Winters to Buffalo for the 1986 season. The promotions began anew for the local hero.

Winters got off to a poor start in Buffalo, however, and saw his batting average plummet to .088. To make matters worse, Matt then was told he would have to report back to Columbus. A day before he left for the International League city, Winters wasn't even suited up for a game in Buffalo that already had been scheduled in his honor—Matt Winters Appreciation Day.

Harpo Hernandez

In 1974, 18-year-old Willie Hernandez broke into professional baseball with the Spartanburg Phillies of the Class-A Western Carolinas League. At the end of the season, Willie bleached his afro, making his

Willie Hernandez with his 1974 Harpo look.

hair look like "lemon cotton candy," as one fan said. He then went out
and pitched a three-hitter against the Anderson Mets, striking out 11
batters while walking no one. The Harpo Marx look-alike also had a
single, a sacrifice and a spectacular fielding play. Manager Howie Be-
dell, a strict disciplinarian, just shook his head when he saw his pitcher's hair. "Willie is doing his thing," he said. "I'll never understand
why these guys do what they do nowadays."

No Minors Allowed

Twelve-year-old Joe Louis Relford may have become the youngest
player ever in a minor league game when Fitzgerald played Statesboro
in a Georgia State League contest July 19, 1952. Statesboro took a
13-0 lead, and the hometown fans started calling for the visiting batboy to bat. In the eighth inning, Fitzgerald Manager Charlie
Ridgeway, who had been on the job only two weeks, sent the youngster to the plate as a pinch-hitter. Relford promptly grounded out to
the third baseman, but he stayed in the game and went to center field

in the bottom of the eighth. There the batboy was even more impressive, making a great catch of a line drive headed for the center-field fence.

When President Bill Estroff of the Class-D circuit found out about young Joe's debut, he was not amused. Ridgeway was fined $50 and suspended for five days. Umpire Ed Kubick, who had given Ridgeway permission to use the batboy, was fired. And 12-year-old Joe Relford was let go from his position as Fitzgerald batboy. "I'se done," the boy said sadly after learning his fate. "Washed up at 12. Whuffo aht thou, justiss?"

The Longest Game

At 8 p.m. on Saturday night, April 18, 1981, Danny Parks of the Pawtucket Red Sox threw the first pitch of the game to the Rochester Red Wings' Tom Eaton. Sixty-six days later, the game finally ended.

At 4:07 a.m. on Easter Sunday, April 19, the game was suspended after 32 innings with the score tied, 2-2. When the game was resumed June 23, Dave Koza singled home Marty Barrett in the bottom of the 33rd inning to give Pawtucket a 3-2 victory in the longest game in baseball history. The official time of game: 8 hours, 25 minutes.

The winning pitcher for Pawtucket was lefthander Bob Ojeda, one of several future big leaguers who played in the historical contest. Also playing for Pawtucket were pitchers Bruce Hurst and Mike Smithson, third baseman Wade Boggs, catcher Rich Gedman and second baseman Barrett. Third baseman Cal Ripken and catcher Floyd Rayford played for the Red Wings.

As might be expected, these participants as well as many other observers had a few interesting comments on the marathon.

Bob Ojeda, Pawtucket:
 "They know in Boston I can win the 33-inning games. I just hope they think I can win the nine-inning games."

Father of Pawtucket fan:
 "The last time we came to a game, we had to leave early. This time I promised we'd stay for the whole game. I had to keep my promise."

Sam Bowen, right fielder, Pawtucket:
"We might as well have sunrise services."

Doc Edwards, manager, Rochester:
"The amazing thing is that our four pitchers issued only four walks in 32 innings, and one of them was intentional."

Wade Boggs, Pawtucket:
"In a game like this, you can have a bad week in one night."

Ben Mondor, owner, Pawtucket (about the scheduled game that followed the 32-inning suspended game):
"In the Sunday afternoon game we were tied, 3-3, in the ninth, and I thought, 'Oh no, not again.'"

Baseball's Greatest Hits

"One of my players, and I'm not saying who, said, 'I wish they wouldn't play that song.' I asked why. 'Because every time they play it, I have a bad day.'"—Jim Leyland, manager, Pittsburgh Pirates, talking about the national anthem.

Star-Spangled Pride

In the 1985 Boston Red Sox yearbook, second baseman Marty Barrett listed his favorite song as the national anthem. And Marty's not alone.

Jackie Robinson, Hall of Fame infielder:
"My greatest thrill in baseball didn't come from any ball I hit, from any base I stole or from any play I made. It came when the national anthem played just before the start of the 1947 World Series, my first World Series."

Pete Rose, first baseman, Philadelphia Phillies:
"It doesn't take much to get me up for baseball. Once the national anthem plays, I get chills. I even know the words to it now."

Jerry Reuss, pitcher, Los Angeles Dodgers:
"Watching Linda Ronstadt in shorts and a Dodger jacket sing the anthem made me realize what playing in the big leagues was all about."

The Baseball Beat

Roger Clemens, pitcher, Red Sox (when asked what music the Red Sox listen to on the team bus):
"Whatever Jim Rice wants."

Joe West, National League umpire and singer-songwriter:
"The first time I sang at Gilley's, when I got off the stage, these two girls rushed me, and I said to myself, 'Move over, Elvis, I'm a star.' It turned out they just wanted tickets to an Astros game."

Huey Lewis, lead singer, Huey Lewis and the News:
"The great thing about tonight is that I'm going to meet Tina Turner. The only thing more exciting than that will be the Cubs and Tigers in the World Series."

Dave Frishberg, musician-songwriter:
"I was present at a Dodgers old-timers banquet to hear Sue Raney sing the world premiere of my song ('Dodger Blue'). I watched a tear roll down Walter Alston's cheek. I knew I had found my calling: To make ball players cry."

John Kiley, organist, Red Sox (after the Kansas City Royals had shut out Boston, 1-0):
"I played more hits than the two teams got."

George Thorogood, lead singer, George Thorogood and the Destroyers:
"Our idea of a party is sitting with a Baseball Encyclopedia for four hours in a bowling alley."

Tim McCarver, announcer, ABC-TV (after interviewing Lawrence Welk):
"I guess we'll see a lot of a-one and a-two counts."

Bob Ojeda, pitcher, New York Mets (comparing the life of a baseball star to that of a rock star on MTV):
"The fans throw different things. Rock stars have nice stuff like flowers and underwear. We get batteries and knives."

Peter Pascarelli, Philadelphia Inquirer (about outfielder Dave Parker being signed by the Cincinnati Reds as a free agent):
"Picturing the flamboyant Parker with his beard, earring and raffish style with the staid Reds and their rigid new manager, Vern Rapp, is like picturing Ozzy Osbourne playing the Metropolitan Opera."

Tom Ludwig, New Jersey baseball fan (in a letter to the New York Daily News):
"I think (Minnesota Twins outfielder) Kirby Puckett should be elected American League player rep. That way, if there's a disagreement in the players association, the headlines could read: 'Kirby Puckett and the Union Gap.'"

Franz Lidz, Sports Illustrated:
"All a ball player has to do to be considered an intellectual is read Kurt Vonnegut or own a Billy Joel album."

Sparky Anderson, Detroit Tigers manager and CBS Radio announcer

(about Billy Joel, who sang the national anthem before Game 2 of the 1986 World Series):
   "Who's he?"

Phillies fan:
   "The owners are paying Sinatra prices and are only getting Fabian."

Discordant Notes

At age 86, St. Louis Cardinals Owner August A. Busch Jr. recorded an album of "Gussie's Greatest Hits." One of Gussie's biggest numbers is "Bad, Bad Leroy Brown."

In 1986, the Chicago White Sox had Musical Headband Day at Comiskey Park. Fans received musical headbands that actually played the unofficial White Sox theme song, "Na Na, Hey Hey, Goodbye."

On July 12, 1979, the White Sox held Disco Demolition Night at Comiskey Park. White Sox Owner Bill Veeck urged fans to bring disco records to the game to be burned between games of a doubleheader with the Tigers. The fans demolished the disco records—but they also demolished the field. The scheduled second game of the doubleheader had to be forfeited to Detroit.

On the April 1986 night that Boston pitcher Roger Clemens struck out 20 Seattle Mariners, Red Sox announcer Ken Coleman mentioned that Clemens' favorite singer was "Steve Nicks." Coleman's radio partner, Joe Castiglione, paused and then said, "Ken, that's *Stevie* Nicks." Coleman responded: "You're probably just saying that because you know him." The next day, Coleman arrived at the press box, and hanging in his radio booth was a poster of Stevie, otherwise known as Stephanie Nicks, the glamorous female vocalist who rose to fame as part of Fleetwood Mac.

Baseball's Own Brand of Religion

"There are three things in my life which I really love: God, my family and baseball. The only problem—once baseball season starts, I change the order around a bit."—Dirty Al Gallagher, third baseman, San Francisco Giants.

It's Right There in the Bible

Baseball and religion go way back, all the way to the start of time. In the Holy Bible, the very first verse of the Old Testament makes reference to baseball. Genesis 1:1 says: "In the big inning. . . ."

Radio station WTIK-AM in Durham, N.C., features an evening program called "Back to the Bible." This religious program usually precedes the Atlanta Braves' games. But when Ted Turner's Braves started playing a number of home games at 5:40 p.m., a conflict developed. The solution: The broadcast cuts away in the middle of the game to "Back to the Bible" and then upon completion goes "Back to the Braves." Honest Injun!

Billy Martin has gotten in more than his share of fights, both as a player and manager. In order to curtail the fisticuffs, Billy was advised—as in the Bible—to turn the other cheek. Billy's retort: "Turn the other cheek? Do you know what I think? I think they must have said that before there were sports."

The Bible even entered the picture when baseball players elected to go on strike in 1981. "Let's get rid of these guys and get new ones," Braves Owner Ted Turner said. "That's what the Lord did. He drowned them all and started over again with two of each kind."

The Power of Prayer

Utilityman Jim Morrison of the Pittsburgh Pirates was most thankful for his game-winning run batted in against the Los Angeles Dodgers and relief pitcher Steve Howe. "I wanted a fastball down the middle," Morrison said, "and the Lord delivered one."

Pitcher Dennis Eckersley also was thankful when he was traded from the Boston Red Sox in the American League to the Chicago Cubs in the National League in 1984. "It's a big difference not having the

DH," he said. "Just when you think you are going to die, up comes the pitcher. Thank thee!"

The Dodgers' Pedro Guerrero discussed his thoughts about prayer in relation to trying to play third base: "I pray to God nobody hits the ball to me. Then I pray to God nobody hits the ball to (second baseman) Steve Sax."

During the 1984 N.L. Championship Series between the Cubs and the San Diego Padres, Father Jerry Sims, a Padres fan, made a deal with a priest in Chicago who was pulling for the Cubs. "I promised I would not pray for the Padres if he would not pray for the Cubs," Father Sims said. "I lied."

The philosophy of Ballwin Baptist Church in St. Louis during the 1985 World Series also smacked of homerism: "Baseball is only a game. Life is eternal. Nevertheless, go Cardinals!"

In 1982, New York Yankees outfielder Dave Collins found out that he was in the starting lineup for the first time in quite awhile. Collins requested help: "Pray for me. I'm not sure I remember how to play."

In 1985, the New York Mets' Ron Darling decided to pitch against the Montreal Expos even though he had a toothache. Darling won, 1-0. "I knew the man upstairs wouldn't give me a bad tooth and a loss on the same day," he said.

Exactly Who Is He?

Pitcher Dennis (Oil Can) Boyd of the Red Sox was asked about designated hitter Don Baylor's importance to the 1986 team, which ultimately won the A.L. pennant. The Can replied: "He's like God on Earth."

On the other hand, when Dwight Gooden struck out 16 Giants, San Francisco's Chili Davis had three hits and didn't strike out even once. Chili seemed far from impressed with the Mets' pitcher: "He ain't God, man."

Kansas City Royals reliever Dan Quisenberry had some shaky moments in 1985, even though he saved 37 games. "I've learned this year more than ever that I'm not God," he said. "I can't direct the ball to the gloves. Earlier in my career, all the ground balls went to our fielders' gloves."

In 1984, Cubs announcer Harry Caray rejoiced in a spectacular double play that ended an important game. "Now I know the good Lord is rooting for the Cubs," he exclaimed.

Cardinals pitcher Neil Allen expressed his amazement at the major league record of 45 saves: "Only God can save 45 games." (Dave Righetti of the Yankees later saved 46 games in 1986.)

The 1986 Texas Rangers got off to a good start despite a poor team image. Roger Rienstra, head of a public relations firm in Fort Worth, discussed the Rangers' needs: "It's a team that needs Jesus Christ playing for it."

In 1983, pitcher Mike Brown disavowed any claim to supernatural status when he explained his position with the Red Sox: "I'm a rookie, not a savior."

During one of his many stints as Yankee manager, Billy Martin had this message for rival Manager Tom Lasorda of the Dodgers: "Tell Lasorda he's going to be shocked when he dies and goes to heaven and finds the Lord has pinstripes on."

Different Strokes For . . .

Whitey Herzog, manager, Cardinals:
   "When I tell a player to hustle and he says to me that God will take care of his slump, I tell him God may do a lot of things, but he don't know nothing about hitting!"

Sparky Anderson, manager, Detroit Tigers:
   "If God let you hit a home run the last time up, then who struck you out the time before that?"

Baltimore Orioles outfielder Pat Kelly and Manager Earl Weaver had different attitudes about religion:
   Kelly: "I want to walk with Jesus."
   Weaver: "I'd rather walk with the bases loaded."

Clint Hurdle, catcher, Mets (about his life after becoming a Christian):
   "I began to wake up in the morning and say, 'Good morning, Lord,' instead of 'Good Lord, morning.'"

Orel Hershiser, pitcher, Dodgers:
   "Being a Christian doesn't mean you have to be a wimp."

Richie Allen, former major league infielder:
   "I'm more interested in trying to get to heaven than getting in the Hall of Fame."

Jerry Reuss, pitcher, Dodgers:
   "If Tommy Lasorda had been cast as the manager in the movie 'The Natural,' his language would have made the film X-rated."

The Devil Made Him Say It

Pitcher Nolan Ryan's position in baseball was clarified by Tigers outfielder Dick Sharon: "He's baseball's exorcist—scares the devil out of you."

Giants catcher Johnny Rabb even scared himself: "I feel as if my arm is possessed. I tell it what to do, then I ask myself why it did what it did."

In late 1982, after 15 seasons in the Dodgers' organization, first baseman Steve Garvey didn't know where he would be playing the next season. "I'm sort of in purgatory now, not knowing what is going to happen," he said.

Yankees pitching coach Sammy Ellis had this devilish evaluation of Joe Cowley: "It's too bad the good Lord blessed him with such a good right arm. By doing so, he ruined a good truck driver."

Religion as a Last Resort

It was Mets pitcher Tug McGraw who coined the phrase, "You gotta believe." But Tom Lasorda is a firm believer in anything that might help win a ball game.

Once when the Dodgers were in Cincinnati, their manager attended a church service and happened to notice Reds Manager John McNamara in a nearby pew. After the service, McNamara told Lasorda to wait a moment and he'd be right out. Lasorda was suspicious, so he kept an eye on his managerial adversary and saw him kneel and light a candle. Lasorda then sneaked back into the church and blew the candle out.

"You do anything you can to win," said Lasorda, whose team beat Cincinnati that day.

The Name of the Game Is Names

"Every time I sign a ball, and there must have been thou-
sands, I thank my luck that I wasn't born Coveleski or
Wambsganss or Peckinpaugh."—Mel Ott, Hall of Fame
outfielder.

Gorman Thomas of the Milwaukee Brewers once was asked to sign a
baseball that already had been signed by Babe Ruth, Hank Aaron,
Mickey Mantle and Joe DiMaggio. Stormin' Gorman added his
signature and then pondered aloud: "There's no telling what that ball
was worth before I signed it."

A Joe DiMaggio autograph is certainly a coveted treasure. But one
time, as Joe got ready to sign his name, the autograph seeker made a
special request—that he sign his name as "Mr. Coffee."

Nick Nick Bo Bick Banana Fana . . .

"I refuse to call a 47-year-old, white-haired man Sparky."
—Al Clark, American League umpire (referring, of course,
to Detroit Tigers Manager George Anderson).

One of the best nicknames of all time belongs to catcher Doug
Gwosdz. Doug, whose name is pronounced "Goosh," has spent time
with the San Diego Padres, San Francisco Giants and New York Mets
organizations, but it doesn't really matter where he plays because the
great thing about Doug Gwosdz is his nickname: Eye Chart.

Chicago Cubs catcher Steve Christmas has the nickname "Tree."
Steve lives just down the road from Christmas, Fla.

Gene Locklear was a rookie with the Cincinnati Reds in 1973. It
wasn't long before Locklear was nicknamed "Pele" by Pete Rose, who
claimed that Gene was always kicking the ball around the outfield.

You might wonder why the Minnesota Twins' shortstop, Greg Gagne,
is called Greg (The Spoon) Gagne? Haven't you ever heard the ex-
pression "Gagne with a spoon"?

The New York Yankees had one of the more interesting coaching
combinations when Gene (Stick) Michael coached third base and

Carl Harrison (Stump) Merrill coached first. Collectively, Stick and Stump were known as the "Wood Brothers."

The trainer of the Bellingham Mariners (Seattle's Class-A farm club in the Northwest League) is Spyder Webb. He's certainly not the first Mr. Webb to be called Spyder, although the spelling does seem a bit original.

It may not be unusual for a player to be named after a spider, but there's one instance where a spider was actually named after a player, Hall of Fame pitcher Dizzy Dean. That spider is officially known as Mastophora Dizzydeani. Its distinguishing characteristic: It catches its prey by throwing a sticky globule rather than trapping it in a web. After zapping an unsuspecting insect with its "pitch," Mastophora reels in its dinner at the end of a silk line.

Will the Real _____ Please Stand Up?

On February 1, 1985, the St. Louis Cardinals traded shortstop Jose Gonzalez and three other players to the Giants for power-hitting Jack Clark. Clark went on to have a big season and led the Cardinals to the

National League pennant that year. On the other hand, the name Jose Gonzalez did not appear even one time in a San Francisco box score. It was not, however, because Jose didn't play. Jose Gonzalez played and played well, but before the season started, he changed his name.

At first Jose changed his name to Uribe Gonzalez. He had a new name, but he still was not pleased. He felt that there were simply too many players named Gonzalez. So he changed it again, this time to Jose Uribe.

Finally, Jose was satisfied. After all the fuss, Giants coach Rocky Bridges hit it right on the head: "Jose truly was the player to be named later in the trade."

The year after Jose Gonzalez changed his name, Giants teammate Jeff Leonard decided that he also was ready for a change, although not quite so drastic. He requested that he be referred to as Jeffrey instead of Jeff. He explained to the writers who covered the team that Jeffrey made him sound more formal. The writers weren't too happy about this request, but they complied. Not only did they refer to him as Jeffrey, but they also gave his nickname a more formal ring. Instead of being called "Penitentiary Face," as was the writers' wont, Jeffrey Leonard all of a sudden was "Correctional Institution Face."

Shortstop Rick Burleson also decided to go the formal route one day while playing for the Boston Red Sox. Burleson approached the public address announcer and requested that he be called Richard instead of Rick. Sherm Feller agreed and announced him as Richard Burleson. But Richard struck out three times that game, and Rick was back in the lineup posthaste.

Cardinals Manager Whitey Herzog's real name is Dorrel Norman Elvert Herzog. Lest he be teased about his name, though, his mother gave him a nickname. She started calling him Relly. Thanks, Mom!

Here's a few more nifty real first names: Silton (Twins pitcher Ray Fontenot), Telmanch (Houston Astros outfielder Ty Gainey) and Sydnor (Pittsburgh Pirates General Manager Syd Thrift).

Billy Martin, the Yankees' on-again, off-again manager, was born Alfred Manuel Pesano.

Bill Skowron, the former Yankee slugger, became known as Moose

Skowron, not because of his physique, but because he looked like Benito Mussolini.

Jose, Can You Si, Si, Si

Although Jose Gonzalez changed his name to Jose Uribe because there were too many players named Gonzalez, he still has an even more common first name—Jose. For example, there's Jose Cruz of the Astros. And there are three Cruz sons who are named Jose, Jose and Jose. (At least he didn't name his daughter Jose. . . .)

Another Jose is Jose Oquendo of the Cardinals. Jose's wife is named Zenaida, and his daughter is named Adianez. Zenaida spelled backward is Adianez.

Going Backward and Forward

Through baseball history, there have been several major league players whose names were palindromes. Whether spelled backward or forward, their names don't change:

>   Truck HANNAH
>   Eddie KAZAK
>   Dick NEN
>   Toby HARRAH
>   Mark SALAS

Can't Anyone Around Here Spell?

Jim Fregosi played all or parts of 18 seasons in the major leagues with the Los Angeles and California Angels, Mets, Texas Rangers and Pirates. Fregosi later was named manager of the Angels in June 1978. He directed the club to the A.L. West championship in 1979 and continued in that post until May 1981. So, you would think that everybody would know his name after two decades of big-league service. Not so!

In 1986, Fregosi was named to replace Tony LaRussa as manager of the Chicago White Sox. On Sunday afternoon, June 22, Fregosi won his first game as the White Sox beat the Mariners, 10-4.

It was a most successful day for the White Sox and Jim Fregosi, but it was surprising that Fregosi went that whole summer afternoon without taking his jacket off. When the new manager finally did undo his jacket after the game, the reason became obvious: The name on the back of his uniform read "FERGOSI." Said Jim: "My ex-wife and my kids used to misspell it, too—until they went to the bank."

The Cubs' Davey Lopes also got a surprise in 1986, his 14th full major league season. Despite playing in the World Series four times and also appearing in four All-Star Games, Lopes received his new supply of bats stamped "Davey Lopez."

Bob Kearney's daughter was born February 28, 1985. The Seattle catcher and his wife, Debbie, decided to choose her name by selecting letters from a Scrabble game. Papa Kearney picked d-a-n-a but didn't really like the name, so they decided to go for one more letter. It looked like Bob was very lucky to select an "i," which fit quite nicely to form the name Diana. Instead, they added the "i" to the end of Dana and named her Danai.

In 1984, Gerald Perry of the Atlanta Braves also became the proud father of a baby girl. The little girl's name was Portia, but when Gerald was asked about the spelling, he confidently replied: "It's probably spelled like the car."

Twins pitcher Bert Blyleven, whose first name had been reported as "Ricalbert" and "Rikalbert" in his early days in the big leagues, didn't know how to spell his own name until he was preparing for his marriage in 1971. It was then that he saw his birth certificate and his name, "Rik Aalbert." (Bert didn't lose too much sleep worrying about the spelling of his last name, either. His license plate made it perfectly clear: "BLY11.")

Shortly after the 1985 season ended, Jimy Williams was named manager of the Toronto Blue Jays. That's right; his first name is "Jimy." It seems that young Jimmy left off one "m" as a prank while taking a test in high school. That was temporary, however, and he stuck with Jimmy Williams until he ran across another man with the same name who, like himself, was managing in the minors. To avoid confusion, Williams again dropped an "m," and Jimy has left it that way ever since.

In 1981, Cherie Blake was assigned to proofread the new Cubs media guide, a task that included checking all spellings. When the guide was finally published, Cherie Blake's name was listed as Cherie Balie.

Confusion Reigns in Names

On September 24, 1984, Kansas City hosted California in a double-header at Royals Stadium. In the second game, four players who had the same first name participated. But all four players spelled that name differently:

Derrel Thomas, PR-3B, Angels
Darrell Miller, 1B, Angels
Daryl Sconiers, PH, Angels
Darryl Motley, LF, Royals

Gorman Thomas won two home run crowns with the Brewers and played in the World Series. Nevertheless, "Even my fan mail comes addressed to Thomas Gorman," Stormin' Gorman admitted. Thomas was fortunate to get the mail at all. At various times, three Thomas Gormans have played in New York alone. All three were pitchers:

Thomas D. Gorman—New York Giants (1939)
Thomas A. Gorman—New York Yankees (1952-54)
Thomas P. Gorman—New York Mets (1982-85)

Well, You Can Call Me Ray . . .

In 1974, the major leagues had 13 active players whose last name was Johnson, from Alex of the Rangers and Yankees to Tim of the Brewers. Eleven years later, the major leagues once again had 13 players with the same last name. This time the name was Davis, from Alvin in Seattle to Trench in Pittsburgh. There also were 19 other players by the name of Davis who played professionally in the minor leagues in 1985, from Bradley in Memphis (Southern) to Wallace (better known as Butch) in Omaha (American Association).

According to highly placed sources, the Davis Debacle was discussed by the major league hierarchy at the 1985 winter meetings. The immediate reaction was that the future of baseball was in jeopardy. Enough was enough! It was time for baseball to act. Commissioner Peter Ueberroth was called in, and he met with the club owners in a closed-door, hush-hush meeting.

The Davis Declaration was born. Ueberroth announced that starting in 1986, all future rookies in the majors would be required to have unusual names. "Can the common!" came the battle cry. "Bring on the bizarre!"

It worked! In 1986, major league box scores featured such new names as Incaviglia, Cangelosi, Lombardozzi, Galarraga, Canseco, Robidoux, Sveum, Assenmacher, Plesac, Portugal, Tewksbury, Stefero, Correa, Kruk, Legg, Fielder, Felder, Guetterman, Bathe, Deshaies, Yett, Oelkers, LaValliere, Cerutti, Nieves, Kerfeld, Eichhorn and Worrell.

The experiment was not a complete success, however. Somehow, a few familiar-sounding rookies managed to slip through the cracks, including six Joneses, two Jacksons and a Smith—not to mention a pair of freshmen named Davis.

The Long and the Short of It

Calvin Coolidge Julius Caesar Tuskahoma McLish pitched for seven teams in his major league career. McLish, unlike Jeffrey Leonard, did not insist on formality. He said it was perfectly fine if his teammates called him Cal.

The same informal spirit also applied to Alan Mitchell Edward George Patrick Henry Gallagher. "Dirty Al's" four-year big-league career consisted of playing third base for the Giants and Angels.

On the shorter side, baseball players also have a response to the likes of Madonna and Cher. The Baseball Encyclopedia chronicles the career of a catcher named Lowe, who may have had a first name, but if he did, he didn't advertise it.

	G	AB	H	2B	3B	HR	HR %	R	RBI	BB	SO	SB	BA	SA	Pinch Hit AB	H	G by POS
Lowe						LOWE, Deceased											
1884 DET N	1	3	1	0	0	0	0.0	0		0	1		.333	.333	0	0	C-1

The Talk of the Team

Rock 'n' roll guitarist George Thorogood is one of baseball's biggest fans anywhere. George would have loved to play in the major leagues, but there was one problem. "I had a terrible baseball name," he said. "You've got to have a name like Smoky Burgess, Mookie Wilson, Spike Owen. The greatest name was Tug McGraw."

The following major league players had no such trouble making their respective squads. For example, take the Love Team:

     1B—Jake Virtue
     2B—Cupid Childs
     SS—Leo (the Lip) Durocher
     3B—Pete Rose
     OF—Sandy Amoros
     OF—Bake McBride
     OF—Beau Bell
      C—Paul Casanova
     DH—Jim Rice
     PH—Rick Sweet
    RHP—Ron Darling
    LHP—Rick Honeycutt
    REL—Slim Love
    MGR—Bobby Valentine

This team even has a publicity director—Lovey Stair. In real life, Lovey works in public relations for the Mariners.

In the 1983 college baseball season, the Fordham Rams hosted the Long Island University Blackbirds in New York City. The Rams, coached by former major leaguer Paul Blair, were not exactly all-American sounding. But they sure were all Italian. To wit:

Vinny Ferraro, SS
Tony Russo, 2B
Billy Santo, 3B
Ed Napolitano, 1B
Mike Stefano, LF
John Blanco, CF
John Maculuso, C
Darryl Porfilio, RF
Joe Vanchiro, DH
Tony LoBello, P

Oh yes, give the Rams a standing "O-vation" because Fordham won the game, 7-6. And designated hitter Vanchiro, normally a poor-hitting pitcher, hit a home run.

And how about this group of major league moundsmen who were obviously born to pitch:

Chief Bender
Darcy Fast
Rollie Fingers
Rich Hand
Bill Hands
Jay Hook
Mike Palm
Jim Palmer

Eric Plunk
John Strike
Jake Striker
Bob Walk
Luke Walker
Jim Winn
Early Wynn

I Can Name That Player In . . .

Paul Householder, outfielder, Brewers:
"I'm a household name, but not a household word."

Tim Teufel, second baseman, Toledo Mud Hens (International):
"If (catcher) Stine Poole keeps hitting this way here and gets called up by the Twins, when Frank Viola pitches, they'll have a battery of Frank 'n' Stine."

Rich Yett, pitcher, Cleveland Indians (to Manager Pat Corrales, who had just sent him to the minor leagues in spring training):
"I asked him if he meant, 'You're not ready yet,' or 'You're not ready, Yett.' "

The Blue Jays have a scout named Wayne Morgan, who lives on Morgan Avenue in Morgan Hill, Calif.

Mike Stenhouse of the Red Sox walked seven times in 16 pinch-hitting appearances in 1986, inspiring the nickname "Sony."

In spring training of 1986, Rangers catcher Geno Petralli ordered some Louisville Slugger bats. The shipment arrived, and the Petralli signature was imprinted on the barrel of each bat. But the signature did not belong to the Texas catcher. The mystery finally was solved when it was discovered that Geno's father, a minor league first base-man before fathering a son he named Eugene James Petralli Jr., once ordered some bats from the same company. So when an employee from the bat company went looking for the proper signature, he pulled the right name out of the file—but was off by one generation.

Marvelous Marv Throneberry was one of the most famous, if not in-famous, of all New York Mets. Marv's full name is Marvin Eugene Throneberry, making him—appropriately—the only Met whose initials say it all.

Bobby Durnbaugh played only two games in the major leagues, and both of them were in 1957 with Cincinnati. Bobby's complete name is Robert Eugene Durnbaugh, making him the only Red whose initials are . . . you guessed it.

The Astros' Class-A farm club in the Florida State League is located in Kissimmee, Fla. The team is called the Osceola Astros, however, in honor of Osceola County. After all, you couldn't really name a team the Kissimmee Astros, could you?

Most of the names mentioned in this chapter are names not easily forgotten. But certain names can be forgotten—sometimes even by their owners.

Phil Rizzuto, announcer, Yankees:
    "Well, hi everybody, and welcome to New York Yankee baseball. I'm Bill White. . . ."

Jerry Coleman, announcer, Padres:
    "Hi folks, I'm Jerry Gross. No I'm not. This is Jerry Coleman."

Who's on First, Second, Third, Etc.

Let's give the last word on names to an announcer who can remember his own. The following poem was narrated by Mel Allen on "This

Week in Baseball" at the end of the 1985 baseball season. It includes
the names of 111 men who wore major league uniforms that season.
Managers' names are included, but no individual is used more than
once.

> The Boys of Summer is baseball's name
> For a group of guys who play this game.
> Lineups change and teams add more,
> But here are some in this year's box score.
>
> There's BROOK and BROOKENS, and BROOKS and LAKE,
> and BASS and TROUT and FISHER.
> There's RAINES and SHINES, and a RAY of SUNDBERG,
> WADE and FORD and FISCHLIN.
>
> The Royals are blue with BLACK and WHITE.
> The Giants are BLUE with VIDA;
> They also have GREEN along with BROWN.
> And the Reds have GARY REDUS.
>
> WALK and RUNNELLS, and HURDLE and LOPES,
> From HILL and VALLE and BOSTON.
> From LaPOINT DERNIER and LONG and FARR.
> Some SCURRY from MASON-DIXON.
>
> There's MORRIS the Cat, and DURHAM the BULL,
> MOOSE and HAAS and GOOSE and ROBIN,
> LYONS and BAIR, and JOE'S a COWLEY.
> WHITEY'S a rat, and so is RHODEN.
>
> There's BUTCHER, BAKER and Candlestick's HAMMAKER,
> A BUTLER, a PORTER and GARDNER;
> KENNEDY, JOHNSON and WASHINGTON WHITEHOUSE,
> NIXON, FORD and CARTER.
>
> CHILI, a FRANK, a BEANE and RICE,
> A STRAWBERRY and a LEMON;
> A HEEP of GRUBB, COOK or FREY,
> At DENNY'S or HOWARD JOHNSON.
>
> PRESLEY, JAMES BROWN, LITTLE RICHARD.
> Man can WILSON pick it.
> A MOTLEY CAREW with SAX or HORNER.
> KNIGHT and DAYETT till Christmas.

LESLEY and SHIRLEY, and GAGNE and LACY.
DON and JUAN, GOTT the WINE.
DARLING and DEER and HONEYCUTT,
Texas with VALENTINE and VALENTINE.
There's JESSE JAMES and BILLY the Kid,
RANDOLPH SCOTT, DALE EVANS and ROY ROGERS.
There's CLARK KENT and STUPER man.
That's LAWLESS, LAW and ORTA.

The season of summer has come and gone.
Now, the World Series is here;
So let's drop the names and silly rhymes.
But WAITS till next year.

(111 poetic names, in order: Brook Jacoby, Tom Brookens, Hubie
Brooks, Steve Lake; Kevin Bass, Steve Trout, Brian Fisher; Tim
Raines, Razor Shines, Johnny Ray, Jim Sundberg; Wade Boggs, Dan
Ford, Mike Fischlin; Bud Black, Frank White; Vida Blue; David
Green, Chris Brown; Gary Redus; Bob Walk, Tom Runnells, Clint
Hurdle, Davey Lopes; Donnie Hill, Dave Valle, Daryl Boston; Dave
LaPoint, Bob Dernier, Bob Long, Steve Farr; Rod Scurry, Mike
Mason, Ken Dixon; Jack Morris, Leon (Bull) Durham; Moose Haas,
Eddie Haas, Goose Gossage, Robin Yount; Steve Lyons, Doug Bair,
Joe Cowley; Whitey Herzog, Rick Rhoden; John Butcher, Dusty
Baker, Atlee Hammaker; Brett Butler, Darrell Porter, Wes Gardner;
Terry Kennedy, Cliff Johnson, Claudell Washington, Len White-
house; Otis Nixon, Curt Ford, Joe Carter; Chili Davis, Frank Viola,
Billy Beane, Jim Rice; Darryl Strawberry, Chet Lemon; Danny Heep,
John Grubb, Glen Cook, Jim Frey; John Denny, Howard Johnson; Jim
Presley, Bob James, Mike Brown, Bryan Little, Richard Dotson; Wil-
lie Wilson; Darryl Motley, Rod Carew, Steve Sax, Bob Horner; Ray
Knight, Brian Dayett; Brad Lesley, Bob Shirley, Greg Gagne, Lee
Lacy; Don Mattingly, Juan Beniquez, Jim Gott, Bobby Wine; Ron
Darling, Rob Deer, Rick Honeycutt; Bobby Valentine, Ellis Valentine;
Jesse Orosco, Dion James, Billy Martin; Willie Randolph, Mike Scott,
Dale Berra, Darrell Evans, Roy Thomas, Steve Rogers; Jack Clark,
Kent Hrbek, John Stuper; Tom Lawless, Vance Law, Jorge Orta; Rick
Waits.)

Winning Isn't Everything

"I'm not emotionally suited for any occupation in which you are hailed as a success if you lose 'only' 62 times a year."—Edward Bennett Williams, owner, Baltimore Orioles.

With baseball teams playing 162 games spread over six months—not to mention postseason, exhibition and winter league games—most major leaguers get used to losing now and then. But for those managers and players whose teams seem to lose now, then and most of the time in between, losing becomes an ugly habit. All that keeps them from going off the deep end is patience, persistence and, above all, a sense of humor.

Musing on Losing

Andy Van Slyke, outfielder, St. Louis Cardinals:
"Every season has its peaks and valleys. What you have to try to eliminate is the Grand Canyon."

Rene Lachemann, manager, Milwaukee Brewers:
"There is so much talent here that even if these guys had just average seasons, we'd be in the race. Unfortunately, the only one here who's having his average season is me."

Dave LaPoint, pitcher, San Francisco Giants:
"If they keep this team together, we could finish 30 games out."

John Candelaria, pitcher, Pittsburgh Pirates:
"It has been a combined 25-man effort. We just totally stink."

Frank Cashen, general manager, New York Mets (after losing to the Philadelphia Phillies, 26-7):
"I feel like I've been through World War III."

Whitey Herzog, manager, Cardinals:
"It's games like this (a 17-2 loss to the Houston Astros) that make you want to see a 10-run rule enforced."

"We've had off days before. We've had off days on days when we played."

"What we could use is a couple of shutouts. But I don't know if that would be good enough to win."

"It's hard to get excited when you're 22 games out of first place. It's hard to get excited, going to a funeral."

Vida Blue, pitcher, Giants:
"We were dead before the June Swoon got us this year. Our ship had sunk and we were a submarine."

Bob Brenly, catcher, Giants:
"God, I wish 'June' and 'swoon' didn't rhyme. If they didn't, no one would've ever heard the phrase. Instead, I have to hear it every year."

Scott McGregor, pitcher, Orioles (after Baltimore lost six straight games to the New York Yankees in 10 days):
"We've got a day off. We'll just put our heads in the whirlpool and come back Friday in Boston."

Earl Weaver, manager, Orioles:
"The more they lose, the more I want to come back and punish them. What a spring training we'll have. Start running at 7 a.m., and they'll still be at it when I'm on the 17th green."

John McNamara, manager, Boston Red Sox:
"We're not panicking, but our tops are blowing off."

Frank White, second baseman, Kansas City Royals:
"Things are starting to look a little better. We held them to a tie for the first nine innings."

Frank Tanana, pitcher, Texas Rangers:
"We've really been the Santa Claus, so far, of the American League. We've just given games away."

Tracy Jones, outfielder, Cincinnati Reds:
"We're fine till we step on the field."

Pete Rose, player-manager, Reds:
"They haven't made a guy that can carry this team right now. If this keeps up, (6-foot-5 Dave) Parker is going to be 5-foot-7 and a hunchback by season's end."

Reggie Jackson, outfielder, California Angels (to shortstop Rick Burleson about his teammate's former club, the Red Sox, who lost to Reggie's Yankees in the 1978 A.L. East race):
"Ah, they should have backed up the truck on you guys, shipped you to the Philippines. You were the Manila Folders."

Pat Corrales, manager, Cleveland Indians:
"When you get beat that bad, you just don't want to get anyone hurt."

Darryl Strawberry, outfielder, Mets (with tongue in cheek about teammate Dwight Gooden, whose 24-4 record earned him the N.L. Cy Young Award, although the Mets finished three games behind the pennant-winning Cardinals):
"That damn Gooden! If he hadn't lost those four games, we win the pennant."

Vin Scully, announcer, NBC-TV (recalling opening day in 1965, when the Los Angeles Dodgers' Don Drysdale pitched opening day in New York against the lowly Mets):
"He saw a banner that read, 'Wait till next year.' "

Danny Darwin, pitcher, Brewers (after losing 16 games in which Milwaukee scored only 21 runs):
"Somewhere down the line, things will even out. It just might be in a softball game."

George Brett, third baseman, Royals:
"If a tie is like kissing your sister, losing is like kissing your grandmother with her teeth out."

On the Road Again

"Once you sign a contract, you're little more than cattle. If they don't want you, they can sell you or trade you, and you just moo and move along."—Danny Darwin, pitcher, Texas Rangers.

Trade Talk

Ellis Clary, scout, Chicago White Sox:

> "I don't know how any deal gets done. Everybody wants to give you a biscuit for a bag of flour."

Tom Brunansky, outfielder, Minnesota Twins:

> "Ninety-nine percent of the guys in the league with no-trade contracts had it in their contract that they wouldn't play for us. The other one percent were already here."

Dann Bilardello, catcher, Montreal Expos (about growing a beard after being traded from the Cincinnati Reds to Montreal):
"In Cincinnati you were lucky if they let you have eyebrows."

Bill Caudill, pitcher, Seattle Mariners:
"I was a Yankee for 22 minutes, and that was 22 minutes too long."

Graig Nettles, third baseman, San Diego Padres (about being traded from the New York Yankees, where he was team captain, to San Diego, where he would be platooned at third base):
"They've changed my title. I'm no longer captain; I'm platoon leader."

"The last time I wrote a book, I got traded from the East Coast to the West Coast. I'm afraid they'll send me back if I write another one."

Mickey Hatcher, outfielder, Twins:
"I'm glad we got Pat Putnam instead of Mike Hargrove. We'll play three- instead of four-hour games." (Mike Hargrove was known as "The Human Rain Delay" because of the time it took him to get ready in the batter's box before every pitch.)

Phil Niekro, pitcher, Cleveland Indians (about pitching at Yankee Stadium for the first time after spending the two previous seasons with the Yankees):
"My first thought was, 'Go to the right clubhouse.' I had gone to the other one so often, and I had never been to the visitors'."

Sandy Alderson, general manager, Oakland A's (about the release of Barbaro Garbey, who had recently been obtained in a trade with Detroit):
"We really didn't want him in the first place. We just took him from Detroit to get rid of Dave Collins."

Ron Davis, pitcher, Twins (about being mentioned as trade bait):
"Flatterized me more than anything."

Ron Gardenhire, infielder, New York Mets:
"I'm being showcased on the bench. They have me sitting where people can see me."

Bobby Bonds, outfielder (about being traded frequently during the latter part of his career):
> "I would like to find a home in baseball. The only thing I've been a part of the last six years is American Airlines."

Jerry Reuss, pitcher, Los Angeles Dodgers:
> "There are three signs that you're about to be traded: One, (General Manager) Al Campanis says there's no trade in the making. Two, (Manager) Tom Lasorda says he loves you like a son. Three, you get your meal money one day at a time."

Claude Osteen, coach, Philadelphia Phillies:
> "I'm not sure which is more insulting, being offered in a trade or having it turned down."

In the Best Trade Tradition

Trades are important on both the major and minor league levels. But they sometimes are taken even more seriously in the baseball craze of the '80s—the Rotisserie League.

In case you're not familiar with the Rotisserie League, it's a circuit formed by amateur baseball fanatics who draft their own players and make their own trades to build their own teams in the league. The success of each team is determined by the cumulative statistics of the players on the active roster. Daily box scores are scrutinized, and the team with the best statistics at the end of the season wins the Rotisserie pennant. By the way, the Rotisserie League got its name from New York City's La Rotisserie Francaise restaurant, where the first league was actually formed.

In 1986, the M-Square Rulers offered pitcher Ron Darling to the Sterno Steverenos but requested two players in return, a catcher and an outfielder. The Steverenos needed pitching, so they offered the Rulers catcher Ron Hassey and a choice of outfielders, either Joe Carter or Lloyd Moseby.

The Rulers wanted to make the trade, but they were not sure about the health of Ron Hassey. The "Chief Ruler," J.D. Glenn, decided he had better find out more about Hassey. So he did a natural thing—he called the Yankee catcher. Hassey told Glenn that his knees were bothering him quite a bit, but he was going to try to finish the season anyway. Glenn then told Hassey about the proposed trade. Hassey's response: "Make the deal."

J.D. just couldn't make up his mind. Hassey was one of his favorite players, but Glenn finally decided it would not be wise to make the trade because of the catcher's suspect knees. The deal was dead.

A few days later in the *real* baseball world, the Yankees traded Hassey to the White Sox in a multiplayer deal. But as soon as Hassey got to Chicago, the White Sox and General Manager Ken (Hawk) Harrelson suddenly cried foul. Harrelson was shocked that Hassey had bad knees and complained that the Yankees had given his club "damaged goods." The White Sox demanded that another player be substituted for Hassey. The Yankees refused, but they did offer to cancel the entire deal. Chicago finally decided to accept Hassey, and the trade was settled.

It would seem that J.D. Glenn of the M-Square Rulers, who did his homework and knew that Ron Hassey's knees were bad, knew more about the major league personnel than Harrelson, who gets paid to know such things. Make that *got* paid; the Hawk resigned his post under pressure after the season.

Travel Agents

Mike Krukow, pitcher, San Francisco Giants (about Mets pitcher Dwight Gooden):
> "I'll tell you, I'll trade where's he's going for where I've been. He's got a great road to travel."

Dick Williams, manager, Padres (after the Detroit Tigers took a two-games-to-one lead in the 1984 World Series, with the next two games scheduled in Detroit):
> "I know we're going back to San Diego. I'd like for them to come back with us."

Glenn Wilson, outfielder, Phillies (about his hot start in home games in 1985):
> "With baseball becoming more specialized, it's just a matter of time before we have a home team and a road team. I'm making my bid to be on the home team."

Peter Pascarelli, Philadelphia Inquirer (describing a nine-game Phillies road trip in which they won only two games and struck out 77 times):
> "Fans Across America."

Darrell Porter, catcher, St. Louis Cardinals:
"Actually, the best thing about playing at home is that you are not on the road."

The City Game

"The best part of playing for the Indians is that you don't have road trips to Cleveland."—Ken (Hawk) Harrelson, broadcaster and former major leaguer.

The Rodney Dangerfield of Cities

In 1954, the Cleveland Indians won 111 games and the American League pennant. The second-place New York Yankees won 103 games but finished eight games behind the Indians. Bob Lemon and Early Wynn won 23 games each that year, and the Cleveland pitching staff had four pitchers who eventually ended their careers with more than 200 victories (Wynn had 300, Bob Feller 266, Lemon 207 and Hal Newhouser 207). Larry Doby led the league with 32 home runs and 126 runs batted in. Al Rosen drove in 102 runs. But the Indians were swept in the World Series by the New York Giants, and the city of Cleveland—still awaiting its next pennant winner—has been suffering untold indignities and affronts ever since.

Cleveland's lack of winning sports teams has contributed to its image as one of America's least desirable places to live—or visit. The city simply gets no respect. That theme was picked up by New York Air, which ran newspaper advertisements in 1986 promoting its service from Cleveland to Florida that proclaimed: "Get out of Cleveland before it disappears." The airline even promoted its flight *to* Cleveland: "We never thought we'd fly to Cleveland. But even *we* have our price."

Sportswriter Peter Gammons picked up the following bit of travel advice from the Texas Rangers: "If you're going to have a plane crash in Cleveland, it's better to have one on the way in than on the way out."

When Tim McCarver played for the Boston Red Sox, he made the following announcement to his teammates upon the plane's landing in Cleveland: "We are now arriving in Cleveland. Set back your watches 42 minutes."

Cleveland is not generally considered the No. 1 stop on the A.L. map. For instance, A's broadcaster Lon Simmons was discussing Oakland's upcoming schedule when he said: "The A's leave after this game for Cleveland. It was only by a 13-12 vote they decided to go."

Cleveland and the Indians also come to mind in certain matters of politics and war. When the United States bombed Libya in 1986, television producer Dean Rosen was amazed at a report that pointed out that Libya's entire navy could fit on one American aircraft carrier. Said Rosen: "Losing to Libya would be like losing to the Indians—the Cleveland Indians."

The Indians' failure to contend for an A.L. pennant since 1959 has led to an abundance of empty seats at spacious Municipal Stadium, which can accommodate more fans (74,208) than any other stadium in the major leagues. A few days after a June 6, 1985, game that drew all of 3,730 fans to Municipal Stadium, the Wall Street Journal reported: "The Cleveland Indians were playing the Seattle Mariners here a week ago Thursday night, and huge Municipal Stadium was populated like Australia."

Municipal Stadium has taken its share of knocks from players over the years, too. First baseman Mike Hargrove, who played in Cleveland for seven seasons, had a suggestion: "There's nothing wrong with the stadium that a case of dynamite wouldn't cure."

Indians outfielder Joe Carter was less subtle: "It's the worst field in the country. Russia probably has better fields. A mine field would be better."

Why, even the music played at Municipal Stadium has brought Cleveland under attack. When the Indians hosted California in 1985, Angels slugger Reggie Jackson commented on the music he heard during batting practice: "That's Linda Ronstadt's 'You're No Good' they're playing on the loudspeakers. Is that meant for Cleveland or me?"

The Indians seem to get blamed for everything. For instance, the decision of all 26 major league teams to go with 24-man rosters instead of 25 in 1986 prompted this remark by Montreal Expos utility-man Wayne Krenchicki: "If it's such a good idea, how come it took the Indians to think of it?"

The idea of being traded to Cleveland has struck fear in the hearts of many major leaguers. At the Chicago Cubs' 1986 spring training camp, outfielder Gary Matthews found a telephone message on his locker that instructed him to call a Chicago radio station. The station was interested in his comments on a just-completed trade that had sent him to the Indians. "That ain't funny," muttered Matthews, who couldn't see the humor in his teammates' prank—even if it was April Fools' Day.

A trade to Cleveland might have meant the end of the road for out-fielder Cesar Cedeno, who helped lead the St. Louis Cardinals to the National League pennant after being traded by the Cincinnati Reds in 1985. When a friend mentioned that he could have been traded to Cleveland instead of St. Louis, Cedeno said: "If that would have happened, I would have quit."

After the 1982 season, the Indians traded outfielder Von Hayes to the Philadelphia Phillies for five players. When Hayes joined the Phillies' off-season banquet circuit, he had to learn a whole new attitude. "I'm not accustomed to being funny and cracking jokes at these banquets," he said. "In Cleveland, we took our banquets seriously and saved our jokes for the game."

Ed Glynn, a journeyman relief pitcher, was thrilled when the Indians sold him to the New York Mets' organization in 1984. "I'm glad I'm getting away from Cleveland," he said. "The Indians wouldn't even give me enough rope to hang myself."

Pitcher Jim Kern, who made his major league debut with the Indians in 1974 and re-signed with the club in 1986 after playing with five other major league clubs in between, offered this analysis of the Cleveland organization: "The first thing they do in Cleveland, if you have talent, is trade you for three guys who don't."

Bill James, author of "The Baseball Abstract," implied that at least some of the Indians' problems could be attributed to Gabe Paul, the club's president for many years. He put it this way: "If Gabe was running a hospital, I'd invest in a mortuary."

Another longtime baseball executive, Phil Seghi, was reassigned to a lesser post in the Indians' organization before the 1985 season after serving as the club's general manager. When it was announced that his successor would not be named right away, Seghi found some humor in the situation: "This is the first time I've seen a general manager trad-ed for a general manager to be named later."

In 1983, Indians pitcher Len Barker was traded to the Atlanta Braves for three players to be named later. Duane Kuiper, a San Francisco Giants infielder who had spent the first 10 years of his career in the

Indians' organization, said he understood why the Indians did not announce their acquisitions immediately: "I presume the names were withheld pending notification of their next of kin."

At one point of the 1983 season, Indians Manager Pat Corrales became so disgusted with his team that he told his players: "I don't want half of you here next season. I talked to the front office, and no one else wants you, either."

Bobby Bragan, who managed Cleveland for part of the 1958 season, could sympathize. "The only thing I know," he said, "is that a three-time loser is a baseball manager on his way to Cleveland in an Edsel."

Indeed, it can be difficult managing a club that usually is buried so deep in the standings, its only hope is for next year. But even that may not be the case, as Expos announcer Ken Singleton said in September 1985 upon noticing the Indians' lowly spot in the A.L. East standings. "Forty-one-and-a-half games back! Cleveland's far enough back that they are almost eliminated from next year!"

Believe it or not, the Indians still have some die-hard fans who remain optimistic despite the club's repeated low finishes. After Cleveland went 60-102 in 1985, Indians booster Ray Nock said: "We're just two or three pitchers away from being a fourth-place club."

Nock may have been right. The Indians posted an 84-78 record in 1986 to finish fifth in the division, and they would have done even better with a stronger pitching staff. Thanks to a 10-game winning streak, the Indians were in first place as late as May 8. Pitcher Tom Candiotti had a name for the club's newfound winning spirit: "Revenge of the Rejects."

Even when someone is saying something nice, Cleveland always seems to get slighted somehow. After sitting out the 1984 season, pitcher Vida Blue said he was thrilled to be training with the Giants in 1985. "I missed baseball so much last year," he said, "that I even missed Cleveland."

Umpire Ron Luciano had similar sentiments about the game. "I live at the ball park," he said. "I love baseball. I am so devoted, I even go to Cleveland."

I Left My Hurts In San Francisco

> *"The Bay Area is the center of devil worship, radical groups and homosexuality in this country. It is a satanic region."*—Gary Lavelle, Giants pitcher.

When Lavelle made that statement in 1981, he neglected to mention that the Bay Area also is the home of Candlestick Park and the San Francisco Giants. To many people who have been associated with the Giants and their home park, that was a serious oversight.

Jim Wohlford, outfielder:
> "The only difference between Candlestick and San Quentin is that at Candlestick they let you go home at night."

Dusty Baker, outfielder:
> "I got prepared for Candlestick by putting down all the windows in my car, taking off my jacket and driving around San Francisco."

Bob Knepper, pitcher:
"You should get caught doing something bad, like throwing bombs at archdukes, for them to put you there."

Jim Murray, sportswriter, Los Angeles Times:
"Only a place that calls an earthquake a fire could call Candlestick a ball park."

Dave LaPoint, pitcher (after being traded from San Francisco to Detroit):
"I felt like the hostages when they let them out of Iran."

Bill Lee, former major league pitcher:
"Now I know my goal in life. It's to go to San Francisco and blow up Candlestick Park. That way, everybody will be happy, (Giants Owner) Bob Lurie will be a hero and I'll be a scapegoat."

Willie McCovey, Hall of Fame first baseman:
"We used to feel sorry for the fans, not for ourselves. We saw them sitting in the stands, freezing at night games, and wondered how they did it. At least we were moving around on the field."

Fran Healy, Mets announcer and former Giants catcher (about the possibility of putting a dome on Candlestick):
"It would be like putting lipstick on a pig."

Bumper sticker:
"Whip me. Beat me. Make me watch the Giants."

Even the Giants' own employees sometimes contribute to San Francisco's infamous baseball image. The Giants' scoreboard operator wanted to acknowledge the local school for the deaf at a game, but when the message appeared on the scoreboard, something was lost in the translation: "Welcome, San Francisco School for the Death."

At the conclusion of the 1985 season, in which the Giants lost 100 games for the first time in their history, there was much talk of the team moving. One new location often mentioned was Denver, a city hungry for major league baseball. A Denver writer summed up his city's frustrations: "We've waited this long for a major league team; we'll wait a little longer. We want a real baseball team, or the San Francisco Giants, whichever comes first."

Although the team stayed put, the Angels' Reggie Jackson said he thought the Giants would not have been missed if they had moved: "All the people of San Francisco want to do is go out to eat and go to the Hookers' Ball."

It should be noted that at the end of the dreadful 1985 season, the San Francisco front office got tough and began a complete overhaul of the worst Giants team in history. One of the first key moves was the firing of Perry Archibald, Gary Iacini and Tokita Tadao. Who were these key contributors to that horrendous record? The team trainers, of course.

Other sweeping changes were made under the regime of new General Manager Al Rosen. Among the most innovative was changing Dirk Smith's official title from traveling secretary to director of travel.

Whether or not any of these changes had any effect on the team's performance is unknown, but the Giants did make a tremendous comeback in 1986. The Giants finished third in the N.L. West with an 83-79 record and remained in the title chase for most of the season. Outfielder Chili Davis made the All-Star team and was one of the team's leaders. Then in September of a prosperous season, Chili expressed his feelings about the city of the new-look Giants: "As far as I'm concerned, they should pack up this team and get the hell out of this place. . . . If I had this team, I'd be an Al Davis—pack it in and go somewhere else. . . . I'd pack it up and take a hike. Adios. Pack it up. See ya later."

Big Apple Dumpings

Now that cities from the West Coast and Midwest have been cited for their shortcomings, let's turn our attention to the Eastern Seaboard and, more specifically, New York City. The Big Apple is not immune to criticism. In fact, some might say that it is rotten to the core. There's no question that New York is a tough town. A trip to Yankee Stadium or Shea Stadium is evidence of that—even for baseball players.

Mike Flanagan, pitcher, Baltimore Orioles:
"I could never play in New York. The first time I ever came into a game there, I got into the bullpen car and they told me to lock the doors."

Goose Gossage, pitcher, San Diego Padres (about playing for the Yankees):
"Driving to Yankee Stadium for a game was like driving to a funeral."

Ed Whitson, pitcher, Yankees:
"My first look at hell was here last year (his first season in New York)."

"A bunch of guys were hollering and cussing that I'd better take my family and get out of town, and that they were going to blow my head off."

Gene Mauch, manager, Angels (about California first baseman Wally Joyner being grazed by a knife thrown from the upper deck at Yankee Stadium):
"There are places I'd sooner play than Yankee Stadium. I've been hit with nuts, I've been hit with bolts, but that's the first knife I've ever seen. You wouldn't have too much trouble killing a bear with it."

Helen Maier, New York City shipping executive:
"It cost too much to send a messenger to Yankee Stadium. They have to take out life insurance and everything."

Bill James, author, "Baseball Abstract":
"If I was looking for Josef Mengele, my first thought would be to check the ushers in Yankee Stadium."

Ron Kittle, outfielder, Yankees:
"Maybe in this town, happiness is that somebody didn't steal your car."

Dave Anderson, New York Times:
"Until recently, Yankee Stadium was always 'The House That Ruth Built,' but now (1982) it's really 'The House That Ruthlessness Destroyed.' "

Roger Erickson, pitcher, Yankees:
"They told me they want me to be in their future. I told them I don't want to be in their future. It's frustrating enough to be in their present."

Greg Larson, Baseball America:
"They're spending millions at Shea Stadium to add luxury sky-boxes. Across town at Yankee Stadium, they plowed up the infield and put down a new one at considerable expense. The money would have been better spent to install metal detectors at every turnstile."

Pete Flynn, groundkeeper, Mets (after New York fans tore up the Shea Stadium field while celebrating the Mets' clinching of the 1986 N.L. East title):
"We have a first-place team and last-place fans."

Bill Buckner, first baseman, Red Sox (while preparing to play the Mets at Shea Stadium in the 1986 World Series despite being hampered by injuries):
"I'm ready to go. Nothing is going to keep me out. You'd have to shoot me with a gun. Then again, here they might do that."

Dishonorable Mentions

Milwaukee:
"I don't like playing in Milwaukee. I didn't go out there for a year. I hated to walk the streets or eat food there. The people don't look right, like they were from London, Jamaica or another planet. I don't like the town."—George (Boomer) Scott, former Brewer first baseman.

St. Louis:
"If I was a free agent, I wouldn't go back there for $10 million. If I had to go home (Kansas City), I'd go by way of Dallas to avoid St. Louis."—Neil Allen, former Cardinals pitcher.

Cincinnati:
"The principal sport in Cincinnati is for people to sit on the front porch and watch the tar bubble in the street."—Jim Murray, Los Angeles Times.

Los Angeles:
"I'd like to raise my daughters where the teen-agers don't have pink, yellow or purple hair."—Steve Howe, former Dodgers pitcher.

Houston:
"This is the only town where women wear insect repellent instead of perfume."—Richie Ashburn, Philadelphia Phillies broadcaster.

Philadelphia:
"Philadelphia fans boo funerals, an Easter egg hunt, a parade of armless war vets and the Liberty Bell."—Bo Belinsky, former Phillies pitcher.

Chicago:
"If they ever have Bowling Ball Night here, I'm definitely not coming."—Jack Aker, Cleveland pitching coach, after White Sox fans bombed the Indians with seat cushions on Seat Cushion Night in Chicago.

Boston:
"Boston isn't a life-and-death matter, but the Red Sox are."—Mike Barnicle, Boston Globe.

Baltimore:
"The only trouble with Baltimore is it's in Baltimore."—Reggie Jackson, former Oriole.

San Diego:
"Tradition here (St. Louis) is Stan Musial coming into the clubhouse and making the rounds. Tradition in San Diego is (former Padre) Nate Colbert coming into the clubhouse trying to sell you a used car."—Bob Shirley, former Padres and Cardinals pitcher.

The Men in Blew

"Baseball's major league umpires agreed to take tests to determine if they're using illegal drugs. But they're still fighting eye exams."—USA Today.

The Wit and Wisdom of Ron Luciano

Players, managers, coaches and fans have been venting their wrath on umpires ever since the game's early days. Baseball arbiters have generally responded with more of the same, but the umpire's voice that most often has been heard above all others belongs to Ron Luciano. The former American League umpire has gained even greater fame with his series of books that offer an unusual perspective on baseball and the umpire's role in it. A sampling:

"Being an umpire is a lot like being a king. It prepares you for nothing."

"If Rod Carew has two strikes on him and fouls off five pitches and then takes the sixth down the middle, I'm calling it a ball."

"The only rule that is simple is the designated-hitter rule, because it was written by umpires. The rest of the rules in baseball are ambiguous."

"My main weakness as an umpire was the fact that I could let a molehill become a mountain."

"When I started, it (baseball) was played by nine tough competitors on grass in graceful ball parks. By the time I was finished, there were 10 men on each side, the game was played indoors, on plastic, and I had to spend half of my time watching out for a man dressed in a chicken suit who kept trying to kiss me."

What They're Saying About Umpires

John Lowenstein, outfielder, Baltimore Orioles:
"If umpires are allowed to throw ball players out of a game, why can't players on both teams, by majority vote, be permitted to throw out a belligerent umpire?"

Bobby Valentine, manager, Texas Rangers:
"They go about their jobs with about as much intensity as guys on a chain gang."

Billy Martin, manager, Oakland A's:
"The best player the Mariners had was the second-base umpire; he blew four plays."

Davey Johnson, manager, New York Mets:
"I can only remember being thrown out of one game before, and that was by a woman umpire in Double A who ejected me for nagging."

Don Baylor, designated hitter, New York Yankees:
"It's not surprising he left the game sick. He umpired like he was delirious."

Mark Belanger, shortstop, Orioles:
"How could he be doing his job when he didn't throw me out of the game after the things I called him?"

Pat Corrales, manager, Cleveland Indians:
"Now I know why your crew does so many of our games. We're the worst team in baseball, and you're the worst crew."

Buck Martinez, catcher, Toronto Blue Jays:
"Maybe he's never umpired a game in which there were fences before."

Dick Young, New York Post (about even the non-working umpires getting a 40 percent raise when the Championship Series was extended from five games to seven):
"Is it 40 percent harder not to work seven games than it is not to work five?"

Phyllis K. Merhige, A.L. office:
"I don't shock easily. I read the umpires' reports, you know."

Joe McCarthy, manager, Yankees:
"Don't fight with the umpires. You can't expect them to be as perfect as you are."

Checked Swings

N.L. umpire Jerry Crawford once tried his hand at officiating basketball, but something was missing. "I made a great foul call," he recalled, "and was pumping my hand up and down, but the players ran up the court. I forgot to blow my whistle."

Pitcher Johnny Allen won 142 games in the major leagues and then became a minor league umpire when his playing days were over. One day while working behind the plate, Allen made a call that infuriated the pitcher. Johnny knew the pitcher was upset, so he conveyed his understanding: "For 20 years, I thought that pitch was down the middle. But I was wrong; it's high and outside."

Dizzy Dean once questioned a call by N.L. umpire George Barr, who simply ignored the future Hall of Fame pitcher. A befuddled Dean then told Barr that as a courtesy, some kind of response should be given. Barr said he had indeed given a response: "I shook my head." Ol' Diz knew better, though, and let Barr know. "Oh no, you didn't," he said. "If you had, I'd have heard something rattle." Barr then rattled off his ejection notice, and Dizzy was on his way to the showers.

Not only does pitcher Nolan Ryan hold the all-time strikeout record with more than 4,000 whiffs, but he also holds the all-time record for most walks issued in a career (more than 2,000). But when the modest Texan broke the walk record, he was quick to share the credit: "I never would have been able to do it without the umpires."

N.L. umpire Al Forman once admitted that he received mail from his baseball constituents. "I occasionally get birthday cards from fans," he said. "But it's often the same message: They hope it's my last."

The weighty responsibility of umpires was perhaps best expressed by N.L. arbiter Paul Runge: "Umpiring is the only profession in the world where you have to be perfect when you start—and continue to get better."

Revenge of the Umpires

In a 1984 Pacific Coast League game between the Portland Beavers and the Vancouver Canadians, umpire Pam Postema ejected four members of the hometown Portland team, including Manager Lee Elia, who had hurled a chair into shallow right field. When Sam Morris refused to retrieve the chair, he was ejected, too. Who was this last victim of Postema's active thumb? The Beavers' 14-year-old batboy.

Said Morris: "All the Beaver players told me to stay where I was. . . . The Beavers pay me, and I gotta do what they say."

National League umpire Joe West once ejected two cameramen after they had given a Mets coach and player permission to use their TV monitor in order to watch a replay of a disputed call.

In the 1920s, A.L. umpire Howard (Ducky) Holmes ejected the owner of the St. Louis Browns from the very ball park he owned. Earlier in the game, Ducky had thrown out Browns Manager George Sisler. Then, when Browns Owner Phil Ball climbed over the railing onto the field, Ducky threw out the "first" Ball.

In 1952, N.L. umpire Augie Donatelli ejected two batters on the same at-bat. In a game against the St. Louis Cardinals at the Polo Grounds, the New York Giants' Bob Elliott was upset over a called strike two and started kicking dirt. Elliott was promptly ejected by Augie and replaced by pinch-hitter Bobby Hofman, who looked at a called third strike and, like Elliott before him, started to argue. So, Donatelli had no choice but to eject Hofman, too.

Bill Klem, the great N.L. umpire, once ejected future Hall of Famer

Pie Traynor—because he was sick, so to speak. Traynor was a gentleman and never used profanity on the diamond, so it was quite surprising to see the Pittsburgh Pirates' star third baseman removed from the game. When a reporter asked Klem why Pie was ejected, Klem explained: "He wasn't feeling well. . . . He said he was sick of my stupid decisions."

In another instance, Bill Klem had no sympathy for someone who was genuinely sick. Cardinals Manager Frankie Frisch once got so mad at Klem, he charged down the first-base line toward the targeted umpire. But before he got to Klem, Frisch collapsed. A doctor was called from the stands, and a crowd gathered around the prone figure on the ground. Klem finally made his way through the crowd, looked down at the manager and shouted: "Frisch, dead or alive, you're out of this game!"

Bill Klem, considered by many to be the greatest umpire in baseball history, was voted into the Hall of Fame in 1953. Although he stood 5-foot-7½ and weighed only 157 pounds, the Old Arbitrator could be quite forceful. Once when questioned what the play was, Klem exclaimed: "It ain't nothin' till I call it!"

Remembering Tom Gorman

Tom Gorman, a longtime N.L. umpire who died in 1986, was one umpire who always seemed to have the proper words for the proper occasion.

Once when umpiring a game involving the Chicago Cubs and their fiery manager, Leo Durocher, Gorman called a Cubs runner out on a close play at first base. Leo the Lip was enraged. He charged Gorman and demanded to know how it was possible that the runner was out. Gorman's response totally mystified the volatile skipper: "Leo, he tagged the base with the wrong foot."

Gorman one time jumped the gun on a two-strike pitch to Hank Aaron. When Tom saw the ball headed for the outside corner just above the knees, he bellowed, "Strike three!" Then at the last second, Hammerin' Hank swung the bat and belted the ball out of the park for a home run. As Aaron circled the bases, the catcher turned around to Gorman and sarcastically asked what he was trying to do. Gorman's response: "I'm practicing."

Gorman was behind the plate for many historic performances in his umpiring career, including the first game of the 1968 World Series when the Cardinals' Bob Gibson struck out a record 17 Detroit Tigers. The record book chronicles Gibson's 17 strikeouts, but Gorman saw it a different way: "Gibson only struck out 10; I struck out seven." Seemed that Gorman recalled a few called strikes that worked to Gibby's advantage.

Gorman also knew what to do when he didn't know what to do. "Anytime I got those bang-bang plays at first base, I called 'em out," he said. "It made the game shorter."

A Game of Inches, Ounces and Ages

(But Mostly Ages)

"Well, as you get older, you slow down and the infielders back up because they've got more time to throw you out at first. At the same time, you lose a little power, so the outfielders move in because you aren't hitting the ball so far. When they shake hands, you've had it."—Paul (Big Poison) Waner, Hall of Fame outfielder.

Let the Good Times and the Old-Timers Roll

Casey Stengel, Hall of Fame manager:
"Old-timers weekends and airplane landings are alike. If you can walk away from them, they're successful."

Mickey Mantle, Hall of Fame outfielder:
"If I knew I was going to live this long, I'd have taken better care of myself."

Gaylord Perry, pitcher, Seattle Mariners:
"I'm throwing the ball as hard as I ever did. It just takes a detour before it gets there."

Bowie Kuhn (about his tenure as commissioner of baseball):
"In the past 14 years, I went from being 42 to 102."

Pete Rose, first baseman, Philadelphia Phillies (after tying Stan Musial's National League career hits record):
"When I got that first hit, I felt like 20. And when I struck out the next three times, I felt like 40."

Reggie Jackson, outfielder, California Angels (about the importance of hitting his 511th home run, which tied Mel Ott on the career list):
"It only means that I've been around a long time, that I'm getting old."

Art Fowler, former major league pitcher:
"I pitched in more than 1,000 (major and minor league) games in 20 years and was still pitching at age 48. I couldn't have done better if I'd lived in an iron lung and gone to church twice every Sunday."

Tony Perez, first baseman, Cincinnati Reds (after going 4-for-4 but
failing to hit a triple in a 1985 spring training game):
"There are no ground-rule triples in baseball, especially for 42-
year-old guys."

Jerry Koosman, pitcher, Phillies:
"My goal is to take the club to arbitration when I'm 50—and win.
That is unless they sign me to a long-term contract when I'm
49."

Hal McRae, designated hitter, Kansas City Royals:
"Having my son (Brian) drafted Number 1 by the Royals
doesn't make me feel old. When they throw fastballs by you
consistently, that makes you feel old."

Phil Niekro, pitcher, New York Yankees:
"I'm going to be a year older, and that's going to be on everyone's
mind. No one will talk about my arm. The big question will be,
'Are the bones going to stay together and will the muscles stay
intact?' "

Pete Rose, player-manager, Reds (about his 45th birthday):
"The only thing this birthday does, as far as I'm concerned, is if I
wanted to collect my pension, I could."

Dick Williams, manager, Mariners:
"Every player who was playing in the American League when I
left 10 years ago is either a coach or a manager or a member of
the California Angels."

Don Sutton, pitcher, Angels:
"I used to pitch, golf, have fun, rest and pitch again. Now, I
pitch, recover, recover, recover, rest and pitch again."

Bob Boone, catcher, Angels (about hitting his first grand slam in 10
years):
"He threw it in a spot where I used to be a good hitter."

Graig Nettles, third baseman, Yankees:
"There ought to be a rule that when the temperature drops
below your age, you don't have to play."

Branch Rickey, former major league executive (about senility):

"First you forget names. Then you forget faces. Then you forget to zip up your fly. And then you forget to unzip your fly."

Satchel Paige, Hall of Fame pitcher:
"The goat ate the Bible with my birth certificate. That goat lived to be 27."

Joe DiMaggio, Hall of Fame outfielder (about being selected baseball's Greatest Living Player):
"At my age, I'm just happy to be named the greatest living anything."

Danny Heep, outfielder, New York Mets (upon seeing veteran bullpen coach Vern Hoscheit in spring training):
"Vern, aren't you dead yet?"

Retirement Fun

Gaylord Perry, former major league pitcher:
"I retired to go to work. How many people can say that?"

Charlie Gehringer, Hall of Fame second baseman:
"Us ball players do things backward. First we play, then we retire and go to work."

Keith Hernandez, first baseman, Mets:
"It's sad you can't retire at 65 in this game like you can in most professions."

Tommy John, pitcher, Yankees (after Oakland A's rookie Mark McGwire, his dentist's son, got his first two major league hits off him):
"When your dentist's kid starts hitting you, it's time to retire."

Sandy Koufax, Hall of Fame pitcher (about Mets Manager Davey Johnson's boast that he had gotten the last hit ever given up by the great Dodger lefthander):
"Yeah, that's why I retired."

Ted Williams, Hall of Fame outfielder:
"I remember one day in September when I was on second base and I looked at home, and I said, 'Boy, that's a long ways.' And I knew it was time to go."

Wheeze Kids

In 1950, the Phillies won the N.L. pennant and were known as the Whiz Kids because of their youth. In 1983, the Phillies again won the N.L. pennant, but this time they were known as the Wheeze Kids because of their age. In other words, 1983 was the year of vets at the Vet.

Player	Age during World Series
Pete Rose	42
Tony Perez	41
Joe Morgan	40
Ron Reed	40
Tug McGraw	39
Steve Carlton	38
Mike Schmidt	34
Garry Maddox	34
Gary Matthews	33
Ed Farmer	33
Greg Gross	31
Al Holland	31
Ivan DeJesus	30
John Denny	30
Bo Diaz	30

Paul Owens, general manager, Phillies:
> "Hey, get me the address of this 92-year-old guy. We might be able to use him, especially if I can't sign Luis Tiant."

Steve Stone, announcer, Chicago Cubs:
> "They may O.D. on experience."

Mike Schmidt, third baseman, Phillies:
> "You know how it is. If we win it, it's because we're a veteran team. If we lose it, it's because we're too old."

Diamond Babes

Joe Nuxhall pitched for his high school team two years *after* he pitched in the major leagues. After appearing in one game for the Reds in 1944 at age 15, making him the youngest player in big-league history, he had to sit out a season of high school baseball in order to regain his eligibility. That debut, in which Nuxhall gave up five runs on two hits, five walks and a wild pitch in two-thirds of an inning against the St. Louis Cardinals, was a frightening experience for the youngster: "I looked back to I guess about three weeks prior to that when I was pitching against junior high school kids—12, 13, 14 years old—and all of a sudden now I've got to face Stan Musial."

Dave Parker (about his first home run in baseball, at age 9):
> "I just stood there at the plate and cried without going around the bases. I was upset because I had broken the bat."

Davey Johnson, manager, Mets (about the 1985 N.L. Cy Young Award winner):
> "The only thing 20 years old about Dwight Gooden is his birth certificate."

Phillies rookie Dave Bennett's 1964 Topps baseball card:
> "The 19-year-old righthanded curveballer is just 18 years old."

Barry Foote, catcher, Phillies:
> "Since I'm only 25, I figure my future is ahead of me."

Ken Berry, manager, Oneonta Yankees (about managing in the minor leagues):
> "Bonus babies can be a real problem for their teammates. I'm talking about attitude. It's not the bonus that bothers you. It's the baby."

Jim Kern, pitcher, Phillies:
   "I'm in great shape. My wife says I've got a 25-year-old body and a 16-year-old mind."

Casey Stengel, manager, Mets (about two of his younger players):
   "In 10 years, Ed Kranepool has a chance to be a star. In 10 years, Greg Goossen has a chance to be 30."

Pat Corrales, manager, Cleveland Indians (about catcher Andy Allanson's tantrum during a game):
   "He had no business acting like a 5-year-old kid. Let me act that way."

Larry Parrish, outfielder, Texas Rangers (explaining why few of his teammates had joined him after the game in the hotel bar):
   "Heck, there are only about five of us old enough to be in here."

To Yield the Right of Weigh

Unlike most major league sports, the baseball diamond displays human beings of all shapes and sizes. For instance, there's Royals outfielder Bo Jackson, whose physique is as incredible as a hulk can be. On the lighter side, there's pitcher Dennis (Oil Can) Boyd of the Boston Red Sox and Cardinals outfielder Curt Ford, who roomed together in college at Jackson State. But their room must have been an isolation cell with rations of bread and water. Together they weigh about the same as Houston Astros relief pitcher Charlie Kerfeld (more about him later).

Terry Forster, pitcher, Atlanta Braves:
   "A waist is a terrible thing to mind."

David Letterman, late-night talk-show host (about Forster):
   "The fattest man in professional sports . . . a fat tub of goo . . . a silo!"

Dave LaPoint, pitcher, Detroit Tigers (about losing 25 pounds):
   "I felt the difference when I went into my stretch and didn't have anything to rest my hands on."

Whitey Herzog, manager, Cardinals (describing a bloop double by Reds outfielder Dave Parker):
   "It was a 125-foot quail hit by a 250-pound elephant."

Bob Dernier, outfielder, Phillies (about batting .160 and weighing 165 pounds):

"If I'm going to hit my weight, I'm going to have to lose a few more pounds."

Glenn Davis, first baseman, Astros (about a batting slump):

"My wife told me I've at least got to get my average from her weight to my weight. I told her I'd like to get to our combined weight. Right now, it's mine and the dog's."

Bruce Sutter, pitcher, Braves (after being told that he looked like he had lost a lot of weight):

"You would, too, if you backed up third base as often as I have this year."

Greg Booker, pitcher, San Diego Padres (about rookie teammate Bip Roberts, who was listed as 5-foot-7, 150 pounds):

"We have baked potatoes back in North Carolina that are bigger than him."

John Wathan, catcher, Royals (about Dan Quisenberry's ability to pitch every day but never get tired):
> "There's no body to get tired. That's like asking a broom if it's tired."

The Weight Is Worth It

Charlie Kerfeld arrived on the major league scene in late 1985, and baseball has not been the same since. The bespectacled heavyweight, a native of Knob Noster, Mo., and educated at Yavapai College in Arizona, landed in Houston almost like a creature from outer space. It was only appropriate that he would be an Astro.

The odd-looking behemoth, who sometimes sports a Jetsons T-shirt under his jersey, was stared at on the mound. Meanwhile, his scorching fastball was stared at—for called third strikes, that is. When the Padres got their first look at Kerfeld, veteran Graig Nettles stared and stared and stared again. Then he finally asked: "How'd you get Denny McLain out of jail?"

Over the winter, after his short-lived debut, Charlie managed to lose 45 pounds. But his 1986 Fleer baseball card overreacted somewhat, listing his height as 5-11 and his weight as 175 pounds. The 6-6, 250-pounder (post-fat farm weight) had to set his baseball card straight: "I haven't weighed 175 since I was in the seventh grade."

Charlie's first full season (1986) was quite successful. Kerfeld appeared in 61 games for the N.L. West champions and compiled an 11-2 record with seven saves and a 2.59 earned-run average. Then in the mass hoopla of the N.L. Championship Series, Charlie was asked if he was intimidated by the hordes of reporters covering the event. The jolly giant replied: "I've only been intimidated by one thing in my life, and it's not human. It's a scale."

Seventh-Inning Stretch

"Dot feller's a regular fanatic."—Chris Von der Ahe.

Chris Von der Ahe has been called baseball's first great sportsman. The feisty German owner of the St. Louis Browns in the 1800s also is given credit for coining the word "fan." The owner of the American Association club was referring to a Browns follower who hardly ever missed a game when, in his German accent, he uttered the word "fanatic." But the accent was on the syllable "fan," and thus was born a new word for baseball linguists.

There have been varying degrees of fanaticism in the last 100 years. Baseball fans have ranged in intensity from those who attend a few innings of World Series games in three-piece suits and designer dresses to Toyko's Katsumi Tanaka. Tanaka was so disturbed by the poor play of the Yomiuri Giants that he set fire to 15 houses in his neighborhood.

Tanaka, like many intense fans, could have used a relaxing break. For years, that break has come in the form of the seventh-inning stretch. One explanation has that tradition starting in 1882 in New York in a game between Manhattan College and the New York Metropolitans, a semipro club. Along about the seventh inning, Manhattan's coach, Brother Jasper, noticed that the students were restless and suggested that they take a stretch. The students made a habit of that exercise, and the practice eventually spread to the major leagues. The seventh-inning stretch was then, and always has been, for fans and fans alone.

Likewise, this chapter is for and about fans, without whom there would be no professional baseball.

Boo Who

In one 1984 game, Chicago White Sox fans booed Manager Tony LaRussa, slugger Ron Kittle, the Chicken, "Take Me Out to the Ball Game" and the ground crew.

Sixto Lezcano, outfielder, Philadelphia Phillies:
"We do so well on the road because the fans don't boo us so much."

Tom House, coach, Texas Rangers (about the time he spent pitching

for the Boston Red Sox):
> "For a year and a half, I never heard my last name at Fenway Park. I heard, 'Now pitching for Boston, Tom Boooooo.'"

Bill Madlock, third baseman, Los Angeles Dodgers (about San Francisco Giants fans at Candlestick Park):
> "Beat us, cheer them, boo us; that's fine. But don't throw chicken bones."

Banner Banter

Memorial Stadium, Baltimore:
> "Hey, Chicago, good thing your city's windy, because your Sox smell."

Royals Stadium, Kansas City:
> "Give me a loaf of Brett, a pound of Biancalana and a slice of Balboni."

Atlanta-Fulton County Stadium:
> "Ted (Turner)—forget CBS; buy us a pitcher."

Fenway Park, Boston (after the Red Sox beat the New York Mets in the first two games of the 1986 World Series):
> "Sox 2, Mets 0, Yankees—no game today."

One in a Million

In 1985, the Montreal Expos saluted the 25,000,000th fan in the history of the franchise. The lucky fan was Fred Morrison. For being in the right place at the right time, he received Expos season tickets, a year's supply of gas from a Montreal station and a one-year subscription to La Presse, the French-language daily newspaper. Only one problem: Morrison turned out to be an English-speaking fan from Toronto—just visiting.

Sounds of Silence

Bill Caudill, pitcher, Seattle Mariners (at the Metrodome in Minnesota against the Twins):
> "It was so quiet I heard a guy in the upper deck burp, and then I heard a woman in the left-field stands yell, 'Pardon you!'"

Doug Rader, manager, Rangers (at Arlington Stadium in Texas):
> "It was so quiet I could hear the catcher putting down the signals."

Jack Morris, pitcher, Detroit Tigers (about San Diego/Jack Murphy Stadium during the first game of the 1984 World Series):

"It was so loud, it was almost like silence."

Dennis (Oil Can) Boyd, pitcher, Red Sox (about Anaheim Stadium during the 1986 American League Championship Series against the California Angels):

"The humming here is constant; it never stops. I don't mean to come out with a Yogi Berra-ism, but you hear this crowd when it's quiet."

Cheers

Every baseball fan has a special hangout where he can meet with friends and discuss the events of the day. It could be a place like Cheers, the friendly bar in Boston on television's situation comedy of the same name, or it could be the student lounge, or around the water cooler at the office. Wherever friends and acquaintances meet, fans can talk baseball.

The following cast of characters is real. The names are unchanged because none is innocent. All stand accused of being genuine baseball fans. These people really exist, and many of them work closely with the author. Let's listen in to what might pass for typical chitchat among followers of the national pastime.

Kenny Mac:

"The thing I remember most about the Brooklyn Dodgers is that they could all spit through their teeth. I used to practice all the time, but all I ever got was a wet T-shirt."

Adolph:

"Yesterday was the worst day of my life; my baseball mitt was stolen. It was in my car. Oh yeah, my car was stolen, too."

"I had a girlfriend, but I just put her on waivers."

The Big Guy:

"I remember seeing the very first Mets game on television (as a youngster). The camera went around the infield and outfield and showed each player. And I remember thinking what a good team they had."

Quado:

"County Stadium in Milwaukee has the busiest urinals I've ever seen. People are so drunk that they keep 'em on automatic flush."

"My dog's like (Brewers star) Robin Yount. It seems like she's been around forever, but she's still young."

Joel:

"I know what a game-winning RBI is. Let me tell you. It's the RBI . . . that wins the ball game."

"You can't do anything about something you can't do anything about." (Is this guy related to Yogi?)

Franken:

"When they showed the Thurman Munson piece on the scoreboard at Yankee Stadium, you could have heard a pinstripe drop."

"Why are doubleheaders called doubleheaders? I've never heard a single game called a header."

Hangman:
   "Atlee Hammaker (of the Giants)? What's that, an accessory for
   a videotape recorder?"

   (On the Mets' catcher): "I think Gary Carter's real ambition is
   to someday become Phil Donahue."

Gulliver (after visiting his favorite team):
   "Some of the guys can hit .300, but when you look at their hand-
   writing and spelling, it's scary. It makes you want to see to it that
   they are not allowed to drive vehicles or operate power tools."

Jacky O:
   "The P.A. guy in Montreal is bisexual. He gives the lineups in
   English and French."

Kimmie:
   "It looked like the Orioles had a dynasty, but it turned into a
   dinosaur."

Domo (about Ozzie Smith's steal of second base in the 1981 All-Star
Game):
   "When (catcher) Bo Diaz threw to second base, (center fielder
   Dave) Winfield should have called for a fair catch."

The Write Stuff

"What kind of character can you have, working for a newspaper? Every reporter is a pitiful pig."—Howard Cosell, sports broadcaster.

Five years after uttering the preceding words, Howard Cosell joined the ranks of pigdom in 1986 and became a nationally syndicated newspaper columnist. Actually, Howard never *uttered* anything, so let's start again.

Five years after *proclaiming* the preceding words, Howard Cosell joined the ranks of piteous pigdom and became a nationally syndicated newspaper columnist. Of course, that doesn't mean Howard was immediately accepted into the sty. In fact, a couple of highly regarded sportswriters had stated their thoughts on Cosell years before.

Red Smith, enshrinee in the writers' wing of the Hall of Fame:
"What do I think of Howard Cosell? I have tried very hard to like Howard. And I have failed."

Jimmy Cannon, longtime New York sports columnist:
"If Cosell were a sport, he would be roller derby."

A World Series banner hanging from a gas station somewhere between St. Louis and Kansas City in 1985 expressed similar sentiments:
"Go Royals, To Hell With Cosell."

Biting the Hand That Publicizes You

Sportswriters help major league baseball players become national celebrities. National celebrities make millions of dollars. So it stands to reason that today's ball player appreciates the modern sportswriter. Right?

Eric Show, pitcher, San Diego Padres:
"Unfortunately, my experience with the media has been that they really aren't very competent in reporting anything I say. Most of the things that are written are complete garbage, about the game of baseball or anything else. I don't trust anything I read in the papers. I don't trust foreign correspondents. I don't even trust our State Department. I have a general rule of thumb: If the press tells me one thing, I believe the opposite."

R.J. Reynolds, outfielder, Pittsburgh Pirates:

"I never read the papers. It isn't healthy for professional athletes."

Rocky Bridges, former major league infielder:
"I know what the word 'media' means. It's plural for 'mediocre.' "

Alan Wiggins, second baseman, Baltimore Orioles:
"That Khadafy isn't such a bad guy. The media's just making him out like a bad guy, like they're doing to some guys here."

John Tudor, pitcher, St. Louis Cardinals (in a crowded clubhouse during the World Series):
"What's it take to get a media pass, a (driver's) license?"

John Stuper, pitcher, Cincinnati Reds (about his refusal to talk to reporters):
"Nobody knows about it because no one has asked me for anything."

Julio Franco, shortstop, Cleveland Indians (about the 1985 players strike):
"This will serve you baseball writers right because you won't get paid, either."

Billy Martin, manager, New York Yankees (about sportswriters who

vote on Hall of Fame candidates):
> "I played with Al Kaline. (Roger) Maris was as good defensively and had a better arm. That's not putting Kaline down; he's a Hall of Famer. But that makes you look at who's voting—a bunch of jerks. And that's why I never want to get in the Hall of Fame."

Paul Snyder, scouting director, Atlanta Braves:
> "We spend upward of $50,000 on scouting, and I don't care to give anything we've found out to a 25-cent newspaper."

Ballard Smith, president, Padres (to writers):
> "Why don't you guys do me a favor and get away from me. You're like a bunch of (bleeping) flies."

On the Other Hand

In 1985, Cardinals Manager Whitey Herzog was named National League Manager of the Year by the Baseball Writers' Association of America. In order to give equal time to the fans and admirers of the sportswriter (if such people exist), here is an example of a baseball person who is sincerely fond of the big-league baseball writer.

Whitey Herzog:
> "That's quite an honor, and I appreciate it. Who voted it? The baseball writers. That means even more. The baseball writers are my friends. Coming from them, I am honored."

Police Story

Mike Lupica, New York Daily News:
> "The sports section needs a crime page."

> "If (convicted felon and former Cy Young Award winner) Dennis McLain has a couple of bad outings for his prison team, will he get released?"

Atlanta baseball writer:
> "I've suggested to my office that we hire one guy to do the drugs-in-sports beat full time so I can write about a baseball game once in awhile."

Bobby Castillo, pitcher, Los Angeles Dodgers (surrounded by writers after a rare victory):
> "I haven't seen this many people since the last car I stole."

Bill James, author, "Baseball Abstract":
> "If a terrorist group had occupied Fenway Park in 1973, sports-writers would have blamed it on the designated-hitter rule."

Scribal Scribbles

Peter Gent, California Angels game program:
> "Baseball players are the weirdest of all. I think it's all of that organ music."

Sam Ogden, Time magazine:
> "The sooner you fall behind, the more time you have to catch up."

Peter Gammons, Boston Globe:
> "The free-agent draft isn't what it once was. Type-A players are barely 'Taipei' quality."

Marty Noble, Newsday:
> "The six runs in the fifth (inning) and two more in the sixth came against Greg Harris, who scattered six outs over nine hits."

Paul Needell, New York Daily News:
> "Potential is always having to say you're sorry."

Mike Lupica, New York Daily News (about reported fisticuffs among the Boston Red Sox):
> "If Jim Rice did hit Oil Can Boyd the other day, it was the first good pitcher he's hit lately."

Bob Uecker, author, "Catcher in the Wry":
> "Every time I sold one of the first books—what did we sell, 20 copies?—well, that means I had to go back and type another one. Got to be a lot of typing."